Riding through
KATRINA
with the Red Baron's Ghost

Riding through
KATRINA
with the Red Baron's Ghost

*a memoir of friendship,
family, and a life writing*

J. MALCOLM GARCIA

Arcade Publishing • New York

Portions of this book have appeared in slightly different form in the following publications: *Alaska Quarterly Review, Apple Valley Review, Ascent Magazine, Big Muddy, Bio Story, Cold Mountain, The Common, Guernica: A Magazine of Arts & Politics, The Kansas City Star, Latterly, Memoir (and), Salon.com, The Sun, Under the Sun.*

Some names have been changed to protect privacy.

Arcade Publishing books may be purchased in bulk at special discounts for sales promotion, corporate gifts, fund-raising, or educational purposes. Special editions can also be created to specifications. For details, contact the Special Sales Department, Arcade Publishing, 307 West 36th Street, 11th Floor, New York, NY 10018 or arcade@skyhorsepublishing.com.

Arcade Publishing® is a registered trademark of Skyhorse Publishing, Inc.®, a Delaware corporation.

Visit our website at www.arcadepub.com.

10 9 8 7 6 5 4 3 2 1

Library of Congress Cataloging-in-Publication Data is available on file.

Cover design by Erin Seaward-Hiatt
Cover photo credit: iStock

Print ISBN: 978-1-62872-869-9
Ebook ISBN: 978-1-62872-870-5

Printed in the United States of America

"I looked around at the rooms that I did not see as rooms but more as a landscape for my emotions, a biography of memory."
—Anne Spollen, *The Shape of Water*

"No, rather, he felt suspended between two worlds, never to truly belong to either."
—Dominique Wilson, *The Yellow Papers*

Dedicated to the memory of Dale M. Titler
1926–2014

Contents

Riding through Katrina with the Red Baron's Ghost

(1970–2015)

New Orleans
September 19, 2005

"Who you looking for again?" firefighter Roy Howard asks me.

"A friend."

"What's his name?"

"Titler. Dale M. Titler."

I'm a reporter riding in the back of a pickup with Howard, hanging on to the tailgate as we bounce and crunch over fallen tree limbs and piles of debris. We're looking for survivors of Hurricane Katrina. Since just after Labor Day, Howard and about fifty other Georgia Search and Rescue firefighters have trudged house to house in St. Bernard Parish, just east of New Orleans and one of the neighborhoods hardest hit by Katrina. They have knocked on doors and, more often than not, broken them down as they searched for survivors. We have found six people. Many stayed because they had no other place or families to go to. Others wouldn't leave because it was their home, had been for years, and that was reason enough.

None of them knew what they would face by remaining. Katrina's winds slammed the parish, but a storm surge of more than thirty feet inflicted the deadliest damage. It swept over levees, tossing boats on top of houses as if they were toys, and devastated much of the low-lying parish of about seventy thousand people.

Among the missing is my friend Titler. Our long correspondence inspired me to ask questions, the first step down a road that would lead to a journalism career and into this pickup.

"The level of how everything was destroyed gets to you," says Howard, a tall, broad-shouldered thirty-seven-year-old from Garden City, Georgia. "As a firefighter I've seen a lot of damage, but not to this degree. You known this Titler a long time?"

"Thirty-plus years."

"When'd you last see him?"

"I've never met him."

"What do you mean?"

"I mean we've never met."

Howard shoots me an arched eyebrow, but before he can get off another question, we stop at a bright yellow house on Angela Avenue. I follow six firefighters out of the truck. Dead quiet. Our footsteps are the only sounds. The avenue and the yards around us are caked with drying mud. A metal plate on the door indicates the owner has a medical condition, but nobody's home.

"I hear something," Howard says. "Dog, maybe."

Another firefighter presses his ear against the door.

"Sounds little."

I look through a window at a large shadow expanding and shrinking, moving through the gray light. I step back.

"It's definitely not little," I say.

Howard raises a maul, hesitates. He runs the tips of his fingers against the looping, curved designs of the wooden door. Old, 1930s or thereabouts, he says. But he knows that if something is alive inside, he has no choice but to break it down. As Howard examines the door, another firefighter, Ned Dixon of Byron, Georgia, jimmies the back door with a crowbar. A bandana sporting the American flag is dark from his sweating forehead.

"Let's bust this door," Howard says.

He lifts the maul again and swings.

The door cracks off its hinges, sags inward, and gives way. The claustrophobic stench of rot and mildew washes over us like foul breath, followed by some kind of pit bull or Rottweiler.

"Back up! Back up! Back up!"

We jump away as the dog shoots through the door and looks at us, whimpering. It feints toward one firefighter and then another and another. He's hungry and thirsty. I have a bottle of water. I squat down, cup my hand, and pour water into it, but the dog ignores me. A firefighter helps me back up. I wipe my face with my wet hand. I'm forty-eight, a good twenty years older than these firefighters, and about the same age Titler was when I first wrote to him in 1970. I was thirteen and had just finished reading his book, *The Day the Red Baron Died.* Before then, I'd thought the Red Baron was nothing more than Snoopy's imaginary enemy in the *Peanuts* comic strip. I didn't know he was the most famous World War I German fighter pilot. I didn't know his death was a mystery.

The book filled me with questions. Encouraged by a determined and curious mother, I wrote to Titler. To my great surprise, Titler answered. I wrote him another letter, and another. His letters prompted more from me, and a correspondence was born that lasted decades.

I was one of hundreds of journalists sent to the Gulf Coast when Hurricane Katrina struck on August 29, 2005. That night, in the living room of my girlfriend's Overland Park, Kansas, home, I watched television images of submerged houses in New Orleans that recalled scenes of World War I portrayed in Titler's book. In the first chapter, he described Cappy, a desolate French town near the bank of the Somme River: *A wall. It belonged to a house that now spilled on the cobblestone street. Everywhere were ruined and demolished structures, remnants of houses, and jagged tree trunks.*

I searched the Internet, found Titler's phone number and called his house, but the line was dead. I found an online Katrina message board and listed his name, but no one, not the police, firefighters or the Red Cross, responded with any information.

More than two weeks later, a message appeared on the board: "9/14/05. Re: Looking for Dale Titler in Gulfport. Did you get in contact with him? Haven't seen him in a while. I think he is still with the MS Gaming Commission."

I called the commission but no one answered. The next day, my editor at the *Kansas City Star* called me into her office. Pack up for Louisiana, she said. I didn't tell her I was going to use the opportunity to find Titler.

Now, four days later, I'm in St. Bernard Parish looking for dead and missing people.

Howard and his colleagues have found ten bodies since they arrived in New Orleans. The dead were discovered in bedrooms and kitchens. Sometimes they were in attics surrounded by bottles of water, a final refuge before trying to break through the roof. It was hard to tell precisely where they had died because the water may have carried them through the house like flotsam before it receded.

"The dead ones I saw, I couldn't tell their age except they were adults," firefighter Eric Ashburn of Chattanooga, Tennessee, tells me. "I imagine they had something, an illness maybe, that prevented them from getting out."

Glenn Dorner, task force leader for Georgia Search and Rescue, nods in agreement. "When you see an entire world shaken up, your personal security is threatened," he says. "We've been trained on critical stress management, but there's no coping measures to get through this."

Among other things, he adds, no one advised him on how to handle distressed pets.

"Be careful of the dog!" Howard shouts.

The dog barks at us, won't stop moving. It seeks an exit from our loose-knit circle. The firefighters step back and the dog dashes through a gap between two of us. It finally stops on the sidewalk, tongue lolling, watching us.

"He's scared."

"The other day one came out like a bullet."

"This one wasn't exactly slow."

"It's starving to death."

"Got food?"

"Crackers. All's I got is crackers."

I follow two firefighters into the house. The soggy brown carpet sucks at our boots; water bubbles underfoot and absorbs the imprints of our every move. We pass through a pink-wallpapered hall where framed family photos hang aslant over an empty fireplace and enter another room lined with more pictures of smiling men, women, and children. Floodwater has stained their silent faces, paling them to ghosts. No wonder: A dark line on the wall marks the storm's high-water level just below the ceiling.

Glasses are standing on a bar that is still stocked with booze. I pick up an overturned chair, the one blemish in the otherwise oddly undisturbed room. The scene here is nothing like a house we had entered earlier in the morning that had been turned upside down from flooding. Sofas were piled against back doors, the ceilings dripped mud, and mold covered the walls like thick green fur. One of the firefighters vomited from the rank, throat-closing funk.

We climb stairs into the attic. I brace myself for what we might see. Is there a way to prepare for discovering the dead?

"That's a first," Dixon says.

"What?" Ashburn asks.

"There's a closet in the attic. Never saw that before."

"Nobody inside?"

"Nobody inside."

Back out on the street the dog has vanished. Howard spray-paints a zero on the wall next to the broken front door.

"Place across the street had antiques and stuff," Howard says.

"I saw a TV wider than my arms."

"House over there still had some good paint. Must've bought the mold-free kind," Dorner says.

Inside empty parked cars, rotted bags of spoiled groceries spill onto the seats. There is no sound on the street except for the creak of a rocking chair listing slowly in the wind next to a truck that floodwaters deposited on a front porch. Kitchen curtains hang like poor posture from broken rods. A wet wind carries the stillness far beyond us.

Is Titler still alive? Did he make it through the storm? Maybe he's in one of the hospitals that flooded. Maybe he's one of the dead patients they found days after the hurricane hit. I've got all these questions and I'm stuck in New Orleans because the roads leading to his Mississippi home remain flooded and impassable.

"Hey."

A man in a blue T-shirt and blue jeans looks at us from the porch of the frayed white house next door. A yellow fence wrapped around the front yard shines in the sun. Music from a radio interrupts the silence and carries loudly into the street from an open window. The man raises a hand and we wave back. A suitcase stands beside him. One of the firefighters talks to him for a minute and then walks back to the rest of us gathered around the pickup. He says the man has just returned to his house for the first time since Katrina struck. His neighbors left before he did. He hasn't seen them. He is still standing in the street as we drive off.

"Nice," Howard says to me. "A survivor."

* * *

I had my first taste of war at home, in the many adventure books that lined my bedroom shelves. War was also in the television coverage of Vietnam that my father watched every weeknight if he wasn't helping me and my two older brothers, Butch and Michael, with our math homework—something we dreaded because he had no patience when we didn't understand an equation—while my mother cooked dinner listening to Arthur Godfrey on the radio. Ours was a typical 1960s suburban clan in the Barry Goldwater mold. We lived in the posh suburb of Winnetka, Illinois, sixteen miles north of downtown Chicago in Cook County.

Butch was seven years and Michael two and a half years older than me. Butch's real name was Charles Jr. but my father had nicknamed him Butch from day one. Butch envisioned himself working beside our father someday. Pop, as we called him, was vice president of Perfecto Garcia Cigars, a company founded by his father and uncles. His brother Manuel, in Tampa, was president. Pop drove into Chicago to his South Wells Street office Monday through Friday while my brothers and I attended school. Our mother stayed home, cleaning and cooking and making it her job, when we were around, to fill in the gaps left by public education by stressing elocution, reading, and writing.

She was born in Puerto Rico. In 1929, when she was twelve, her mother died of influenza. A Barbados-born nanny, Amy Clairmonte, helped raise her and her two older siblings. Amy had learned English working for British families in Bridgetown, and passed on her precise diction to my mother. Her influence never waned. My mother corrected my brothers and me whenever we slipped into vernacular.

"Gonna? What's gonna?" she'd say. "It's going to. Now, sit up straight, elbows off the table."

"Haveta? What's haveta? It's have to. Don't slouch."

"Gotta? What's gotta? It's got to. Tuck in your shirt."

She also required us to read a book a week and then write a report. If I didn't understand a word, she handed me a dictionary. If I had other questions, she pointed me toward our collection of red

World Book volumes or drove me to the Winnetka Public Library. She expected me to find answers to my questions.

Every day after school, she had a sentence for us. I recall one: *The fireman parked his truck in front of a burning house.* We then had to compose a story around that sentence. She was checking for spelling, grammar and handwriting, yes, but she wanted more.

"Where are the people?" she would ask. "Who are they? What do they look like? What's the story?"

By the time I was thirteen, I was ready to buy my own books. I had read nearly everything handed down to me by Butch and Michael, advancing from Doctor Dolittle to *Tarzan of the Apes* to the Hardy Boys to biographies of Henry Stanley, Richard Burton, and other explorers. I walked into Winnetka, my pockets filled with an accumulation of my ten-cents-a-week allowance money, and stopped at The Booksmith.

The Booksmith has long since closed, and now the old white brick building on Chestnut Street houses Denim & Soul, a women's clothing store. E. B. Taylor & Company, a hardware store across the street, has been converted into Neapolitan Collection, another high-end women's apparel outlet. When I visit these days, however, I am still taken back to the way it was when I was a child and an A&P grocery store stood a few blocks away. Bells rang as I pushed open the doors of The Booksmith. Slats of gray light shone through the shades of its windows and spools of dust turned above my head. It smelled of books, a kind of closed-in attic odor that made me feel I had entered another time. A pleasant, gray-haired woman with black-rimmed glasses asked if she could help me.

"No, thank you. I'm just looking," I said, mimicking how my mother always answered that question when she shopped.

I browsed a shelf of biographies and noticed *The Day the Red Baron Died*. A photograph of a young man peered out at me from an oval frame on the glossy black cover. His deep eyes held me. The raised collar of his coat wrapped around his neck contributed to his stern look, as did his military cap slanted to one side. His name was Baron Manfred von Richthofen, a renowned German fighter pilot of World War I. He shot down eighty Allied planes—more planes than any other fighter pilot at the time. He was killed in action at the age of twenty-five while chasing a British plane far behind Allied lines, something he had warned his fellow pilots against. No one knew who shot him down. Was it a Canadian fighter pilot? Or could it have been Australian and British antiaircraft gunners? The book promised an answer.

I saw no photo of the author, Dale M. Titler, but a blurb on the back cover said that Titler had learned to fly in Pennsylvania on an airfield named after an associate of Amelia Earhart. He had piloted open-cockpit airplanes and liked to skydive on Sunday afternoons. He had served in the Army Air Forces during World War II. He lived in Gulfport, Mississippi.

To be perfectly candid, what happened on that crisp spring morning in 1918 was a rather simple act of war, I read at the end of the preface. *An experienced—and tired—fighter pilot violated his own tactical concept, and paid the price.*

That sounded terribly romantic to me. I bought the book for $1.25 and walked home. My mother thought *The Day the Red Baron Died* would be too detailed and dry to hold my interest and scolded me for wasting my money, but I began reading it that afternoon, sprawled on my bed, a pillow propping up my head. I read for hours, until my mother called me for dinner. By the time I put the book down, I'd come to realize that Richthofen was once a boy like me who also had a desire for adventure.

He was born in 1892 in Breslau, Germany. His father was a reserve major in the army. The boy *harbored a quiet dislike for discipline.* He never questioned the decisions of his parents *nor complained to them.*

He enjoyed playing in the woods, spending *happy, carefree hours stalking prey in the shadows of dense forests.* He was *a strong, wiry lad* who was *absolutely honest; he was determined to excel in whatever he chose to do.*

Richthofen was my age when he climbed a water tower by way of a lightning rod and tied his handkerchief to the top. *I remember exactly how difficult it was to balance on the gutters,* the author quoted from Richthofen's autobiography. *Ten years later, I saw the handkerchief still tied high in the air.* I tried to emulate his feat by climbing a tree to reach the top of my junior high school. I had no handkerchief, however, and before I got very far, Mr. Monroe, an eighth-grade teacher, told me to come down.

At the beginning of World War I, Richthofen joined a cavalry unit. Bored by the slow pace of trench warfare, he joined the "flying service" in 1915.

Like other restless fighting men his eyes turned skyward to the German and Allied air machines that droned idly over the battlefield, Titler wrote. *He envied them; at least they could see the tide of combat.*

Every time he shot down a plane, Richthofen bought a two-inch-high silver trophy cup to commemorate the event. His squadron with its tents and equipment moved from base to base to be on the front lines. The pilots painted their planes bright colors. Richthofen himself flew a red Fokker triplane, hence the name Red Baron. The squadron became known as "The Flying Circus."

Fame was his, Titler wrote about Richthofen. *He could have had gaiety and the attentions of any admirer he chose, yet he preferred to hunt alone in the shadowy forest, enjoy the companionship of his dog, Moritz—and practice the art of soldiering. What made him tick? Why was he so deadly? How is it, someone will ponder, that his name still grips the attention of all manner of people?*

Back in my room after dinner, I imagined what it would be like to have someone speak of me as Lt. Karl August von Schoenbeck spoke of Richthofen: *He had a noble way of speech and never swore or used foul language of any kind. . . . He shone with calm in the most critical moments.*

It would be something to be Richthofen, I thought. To be called the Red Baron. To be that famous. To be bigger than life. To live in a way that was exciting and so different from everyone else. Sports defined boys my age and I was not good at any of them. I had asthma. I was not a fast runner and often struck out when playing baseball. My friends rarely asked me to play football and soccer. However, alone in my bedroom, I could see myself flying and being the Red Baron. Soaring aloft, shooting down my enemies, leading a squadron I'd call the Bald Eagles. I decided that if the Vietnam War lasted long enough, I would become a fighter pilot.

About a week after I finished *The Day the Red Baron Died*, my mother showed me a story in the *Chicago Tribune* headlined "The Red Baron's Granddaughter." It was about a German model who claimed that Richthofen was her grandfather. Yet Titler had written that Richthofen had never married. My mother suggested that I ask him about the story. How? I wanted to know. She told me to write to him in care of the publisher. That night, with her help, I drafted a letter.

October 22, 1970
Dear Mr. Titler,
In reading your book, The Day the Red Baron Died, *which was a very good book from which I learned many things, I understand the Red Baron never married.*

I reconsidered and wrote above the first sentence, *I am 13 years old.* I then continued, describing the *Tribune* article and the woman who claimed to be Richthofen's granddaughter. *I think the woman is a fake,* I wrote, and then crossed out the sentence and began again: *I would like to know from you if this woman is pretending to be the Red Baron's granddaughter.* After some additional thought, I added *or not.*

About a month later, I received a reply. Butch snatched the letter from me and held it above his head, and I chased him around the house until he relented and gave it to me. I hurried to my room and ripped open the envelope, tearing a "Victory Over Communism" sticker Titler had used to seal it.

November 25, 1970
Dear Malcolm,
Many thanks for your letter. I much appreciate your kind words and am pleased to know you enjoyed The Day the Red Baron Died.

Titler assured me that the woman in the article was not the Red Baron's granddaughter. Richthofen, he explained, was a common German name, and he thought the reporter had incorrectly assumed the model was related to the von Richthofen of Red Baron fame.

I read the letter several times, especially the end, where he thanked me again for writing. He said he appreciated my interest and confidence in his work. I taped it to the draft version of my letter and put it in my desk.

*   *   *

September 16, 2005
Dear Mr. Titler: I arrived in Baton Rouge late this afternoon. I rented an SUV and drove to my editor's office not far from the airport. He said he had an assignment for me and pointed to a desk. I sat down and waited. He appeared flustered. He was trying to get answers about the condition of patients in New Orleans hospitals. He answered two phones at once, holding the receivers against both of his ears. He'd hang up, the phones would ring again and he'd answer them two at a time. He soon forgot about me. After an hour, I wrote a note telling him I

was going to New Orleans. I gave it to him and left. He barely noticed. He was still shouting into the phones as I walked out of the door.

I got on Interstate 10 and drove south. Before I left Kansas City, I had arranged to live in an RV. It belongs to a couple in Gramercy, Louisiana, a town about sixty miles outside of New Orleans. The RV has room for three people. A Star *photographer, Norman Ng, and a reporter with the* Fort Worth Star-Telegram *are already there. My bunk will cost one hundred dollars a night, meals included. A disaster can be a money-making proposition for those who know how to cash in. I'll have access to the couple's kitchen. I'll be able to connect with the Internet through a phone jack. No wireless yet because of damage from the storm. Evacuees and aid workers occupy all the hotels and motels for miles around. I was lucky to find the RV.*

"I'm on my way," I told Norman.

The drive to Gramercy took forever. Convoys of military trucks and Jeeps hauling Porta-Potties took up all lanes; ambulances and police cars followed. Helicopters hovered overhead. The day was overcast and hot. A wet, clingy kind of heat. Families sat outside motels in T-shirts and underwear, the humidity settling over them like another layer of clothing. They glanced up at the choppers, hands cupped over their eyes, squinting against the glare. Seeing nothing, they turned to look at the line of aid vehicles inching past.

Through my open window I could hear the static of battery-powered radios, the scratchy volume like the buzz of insects. Boys dragged twigs on the pavement and played as if they were on a family outing, while their exhausted parents held bottles of water against their foreheads and watched them chase one another without really seeing them, their empty stares never wavering from whatever they were really thinking about.

I stopped at a McDonald's for coffee. It was packed with people who had fled New Orleans. They shouted into their cell phones, pleading with someone on the other end to rent them apartments sight unseen. They offered one thousand, two thousand, three thousand dollars a month and higher. Pacing. Back and forth, back and forth, spilling their drinks, phones pressed against an ear and a shoulder, working off their frustration with sharp jabs and flustered waves of their hands. They paid for their meals while still talking in a line that stretched out the door, their pleadings as a whole rising in one undecipherable and desperate clamor. A line stretched out the door. I was reminded of refugee camps in Afghanistan, the long wait families endured for food, the confused faces of their children and the sense of defeat in the faces of everyone. In December 2001, I decided to play social worker in Kabul and brought rice to a family I'd seen living in an empty, mortared building downtown. Other homeless families mobbed me, and the rice was ripped from my hands. I remember the dank smell of the place, of fingers clutching at me and of distorted faces shouting in a language I did not understand. My driver and I fled to his car, chased by a despairing mob. I don't recall ever having felt so scared and helpless.

At the McDonald's, I decided a cup of coffee wasn't worth the kind of wait facing me. I left and rejoined the slow procession south, passing more motels with more half-naked families sitting outside in the putrid heat. An hour later I took the turnoff for Gramercy.

My new home, the RV, stood at the end of Magnolia Street not far from a Winn-Dixie supermarket. Norman was outside taking photos, his lean body heavy with camera gear. I parked, got out and we slapped our palms in a high five. We were both exultant about being out of Kansas City and working the biggest story of our lives since 9/11 and the start of the second Iraq war.

In Gramercy, Norman told me, Katrina was like a bad thunderstorm. It rained hard and the power went out for a while but that was it. Some trees fell and branches blocked a few driveways, but not a whole lot more. As Norman spoke, I heard the cough of a lawn mower and noticed the flicker of a TV through the open curtain of a house. Nothing out of the ordinary. The only complaint Norman heard from neighbors: mail had not been delivered in days. He warned me that cell phone usage was erratic at best: sometimes you'll get a signal, most of the time you won't.

Borrowing Norman's satellite phone, I called your house, Mr. Titler, but no one answered. I unpacked my sleeping bag and spread it on a cot in the rear of the RV. It's been a long day. I'll try you again tomorrow.

* * *

Although Titler had settled the matter of Richthofen's granddaughter to my satisfaction, I still had more questions. In my next letter, I asked him if he knew where I could buy a copy of *The Red Knight of Germany*, one of the first English biographies of Richthofen published in 1930. Titler had listed the book in the bibliography of *The Day the Red Baron Died*. He compared *The Red Knight of Germany* to a cheap dime novel. I liked the title, however, and, mindful of my limited budget, I told him I wanted a paperback edition.

December 18, 1970
Dear Malcolm,
It's good to hear from you again. Getting a paperback edition of The Red Knight of Germany *might be something of a problem. It was quite a few years ago that I saw it in the paperback edition and I hope it's still available.*

Titler suggested I contact five used bookstores, including Bohemia Bookshop in Sussex, England, where I found a first edition, red clothbound copy for six dollars. It arrived wrapped in brown paper bearing blue stamps with the image of Queen Elizabeth II. The bookshop owner, Frank Letchford, called me "Master Malcolm." I liked that. Opening the package, I inhaled aromas of long ago. I liked that too.

He killed one hundred men in individual combat, the author, Floyd Gibbons, wrote, *shot them, burned them, crushed them, hurled their bodies down to earth.*

Richthofen, I knew, did not kill one hundred men, but I didn't care. I enjoyed the mythic suggestiveness of the overwrought sentences and finished the short book in hours.

I didn't write to Titler again until March 1971, after I'd spent a day with my friend Tom. He enjoyed reading history too, and I showed him my copy of *The Day the Red Baron Died*. We leafed through it examining photographs arranged together in the center of the book. One picture, of Alfred G. Franklyn of the 110th Section of F Anti-Aircraft Battery, Royal Garrison Artillery, caught our attention. He stood beside his gun with his head tipped back, helmet pushed off his forehead, mouth open, squinting into the sky. He claimed to have killed Richthofen. According to Titler, however, Richthofen was too far from Franklyn's position for him to have fired the fatal shot.

Studying the photograph, Tom said Franklyn should have been a conscientious objector instead of a soldier. Tom's parents opposed the Vietnam War. I disagreed, arguing from the point of view of my parents: The United States fights wars to spread democracy. Allied soldiers during World War I were on the side of freedom. Tom and I argued until we couldn't remember any more of our parents' opinions.

Looking back on that afternoon, I understand that we were two boys mimicking the adults in our lives who had been confronted by a war they didn't understand. The TV images of dead and dying American soldiers in Vietnam defied the patriotic, even mawkish, depiction of conflict they'd grown to believe in their youth during World War II. For some of them, the shock of Vietnam led them to protest the war. Others, like my parents, dug deeper into their belief that every war involving the United States was just and good and deserved their support. Children like Tom and I inherited our parents' ideas without thought; without a clue. In all likelihood we would pass on our no-gray-areas beliefs to our own children. So it goes from one generation to the next.

After Tom and I parted, I walked home and wrote to Titler about Franklyn. I wanted to know why he persisted in thinking he had killed Richthofen when the evidence showed he had not. Titler responded two weeks later with Franklyn's address. I understood his unwritten suggestion: I should ask him. Titler also enclosed some of the white-and-blue "Defeat Communism" stickers he affixed to his letters. I had told him my parents appreciated his politics.

March 30, 1971
Dear Malcolm,
Here is Sergeant-Major Franklyn's U.K. address. When you write to him please give him my warmest regards. As to your other question, I'm afraid I don't really know why the Germans were called "Jerries" in World War One, but I imagine Mr. Franklyn could tell you. If you find out let me know, I've often wondered about it myself. Warm regards, Malcolm, and all best wishes, Dale M. Titler.

I folded his letter and put it back in the envelope. Then I took a piece of notebook paper and drafted a note to Franklyn. I used stationery to write the final copy. I told Franklyn my age and that I was very interested in the "controversial death" of the Red Baron. I understood, I continued, that he thought he had killed Richthofen. In a postscript I added, "I got your address from Dale M. Titler who asked me to give you his warm regards, so, warm regards from Dale M. Titler!" I sealed the envelope and walked to the Winnetka post office.

* * *

September 19, 2005
Dear Mr. Titler,
This morning I made my first trip into New Orleans. I'd not gone far when I stopped at a National Guard checkpoint on eastbound I-10.

The guard turned away drivers ahead of me. Only the military, aid workers, reconstruction teams, police, and reporters can enter the city. A young guard member checked my press ID. He grinned in a self-conscious way, still getting used to his role, his authority.

"Thank you, sir," he said and waved me through.

The incident triggered a memory: Afghan soldiers used rope stretched across a road to stop traffic. The commanding officer would demand ID from my driver, Khalid, and then ask for money, usually just a few dollars. His handful of men, meanwhile, requested baksheesh, a tip, from me. I ignored them and waited for Khalid to pay the bribe. When the commander waved us through, I reimbursed Khalid and counted what money I had left to be sure we had enough to pay the bribe at the next checkpoint.

I didn't bother to share this memory with the National Guardsman, although it crossed my mind that he may have served in Afghanistan. Certainly I met quite a few guardsmen over there, but I was well past him when this occurred to me. I drove onto I-10, its flat expanse snaking ahead of me gray and vacant. A damp wind whipped around my SUV and across what looked to me like flattened swamps. Fallen trees formed rails across the ground as if someone had deliberately placed them in rows so many feet apart, their broken trunks splintered like rotted mouths of teeth mere inches above grassy floodwaters filled with debris.

I was alone except for the few military jeeps racing past me. Vacant buildings ripped to shreds, entire floors gone, stood exposed on both sides of the interstate, their empty windows like eyes staring at nothing. Miles and miles of these ruins stretched past me as far as I could see until they became tiny blurred squares merging into the horizon.

I continued driving for what felt like miles and saw no one. Even the jeeps had stopped passing me. I felt I had fallen under a spell, the emptiness and overcast skies hypnotic, and I missed my exit. I made a U–turn and drove back the way I had come. A police car passed me, and the officer waved and I waved back; old laws suspended in a deserted city. I experienced a little boy's joy as I drove in a manner I would never get away with anywhere else. Piles of chairs and discarded clothing had collected beside the interstate, the remains of what people had taken with them when they fled New Orleans on foot. An old man slept in a cardboard box. Was he homeless or a Katrina refugee? Homeless now.

I turned onto Franklin Avenue. The stoplights didn't work, and I raced through empty intersections into a world organized by a cubist sculptor. Boats sat on top of houses. Cars stood upright on their bumpers against trees. Dogs barked from the roofs of pickups stranded on traffic islands. Receding water formed moats around houses.

Back in Kansas City, I had listened to newscasters describing New Orleans as a war zone. Today I thought that was a poor description. The quiet struck me as that of a ghost town, the smashed windows and entryways open in dark, silent screams. I could imagine how it had been before the hurricane. People moving about, traffic. I could feel them on the sidewalks and in their cars. Yet I saw no one.

On St. Claude Avenue, in the Ninth Ward, I noticed the open front door of Mike's Food Store. A shovel leaned against the building. I stopped to speak to a man carrying stuffed garbage bags to the curb. His name was Hai Pham, and he was a Korean immigrant. His clothes hung off him heavy from the sweat of his labor. Pham told me he didn't understand the senseless, willful destruction of his store, and he never would. Yes, he knew why people would steal food and water, even beer and liquor. But to overturn shelves, demolish a freezer and steal his money? No. He could not understand that.

"How do you know it wasn't the storm that did all that?" I asked.

Pham didn't answer. He balled his hands into fists and wiped his eyes.

"Whatever they needed, they could have taken," he said.

Pham led me into his store. We stepped into ankle-deep packages of crackers, spoiled meat and fruit.

"They did not have to do this."

Maybe Pham needed to believe that vandals had ransacked his store because he couldn't comprehend the destructive power of the storm. He could picture vandals. Vandals were people, a tangible image. They could be arrested and charged. How was he to hold a storm accountable? Or, I wondered, had he lost his mind?

"I'm sorry," I said.

He ignored me, muttering to himself as he walked away to grab another trash bag.

OK, now this was like a war. The insensible talk of the shell-shocked. In Kabul, one old man told me that when the Russians came to his village, Mendrowr, in Laghman Province, they lined up thirty-two young men they thought were guerrilla fighters and shot them. Then the Russians detained men they thought might have been the boys' fathers and asked them about their sons.

Where are their friends? the Russians demanded.

The men wouldn't answer, and the Russians executed them too. Women took care of the dead. There weren't enough men left to bury them. The old man kept repeating "Not enough men left to bury them, not enough men left to bury them," as if he worried that by not doing so, I would not appreciate the horror of what he described, that I would forget. All these years later, I remember. "Not enough men left to bury them," like a song I can't get out of my head.

I got back into my SUV, drove past a Civil War statue of a Confederate soldier, and merged onto St. Charles Avenue. Nineteenth-century mansions with white columns and wraparound porches rose up on both sides of the street. Threats warning looters covered plywood sheets: You will be shot. You're no better than carpetbaggers. You must die.

I pulled to the side of the road to use a Porta-Potty. When I came out, I saw a jeep parked by my car. A member of the National Guard stepped out and asked for my identification. I showed him my press badge.

"Thank you, sir."

I watched him leave. The humid air layered my shoulders with its weight. Wind without sound brushed against me. I didn't even hear the scratch of blown leaves against the pavement. No one around. I rested my arms on the roof of the SUV and wondered what to do next. I needed to hunt up a story for my editor. Maybe Pham. He'd be a good feature. Go back to him or keep driving? I wondered if he'd still be there. And I wondered where you were, Mr. Titler.

* * *

Alfred Franklyn had answered my letter. Within three weeks of writing to him, I received a blue envelope from England. Aerogramme / Par Avion, it read. I opened it along its edges until it unfolded into one long sheet. At the top it read, *Re Baron von Richthofen*. A note followed.

April 11, 1971
Dear Malcolm,
Alfred Franklyn here. Thanks for your letter received. In reply I am sending you a copy of my first report I made after I read that a Canadian pilot had brought the Baron down which was impossible.

Franklyn then copied the report he had filed with his commanding officer on April 21, 1918, the day Richthofen died. After he had seen the German's red Fokker triplane behind Allied lines Franklyn *immediately went to my Lewis gun which I had on a mount and fired at him at close range about 27 rounds. I then saw him crash to the ground about 200 yards from my position. There were also two Australian sergeants standing beside me and one remarked, 'You have got him digger,' and I said, 'Yes, he is down alright.'*

Franklyn did not know why the Germans were called "Jerries," just that they always were, and the French, he said, were called "froggies."

Rheumatism in his hands, he continued, made writing difficult, and he apologized for the short note. I held the flimsy paper in my hand and imagined him folding it on his desk in his Birmingham home. I looked up Birmingham in our encyclopedia. Then I taped Franklyn's letter to the draft copy of my note to him and put both in a shoebox with my correspondence from Titler.

April 26, 1971
Dear Mr. Titler,
Mr. Franklyn answered me. Now I shall quote a sentence out of the letter that you will like; 'Kindest regards to you and Dale Titler should you write him or see him.' If you could would you please tell me where I could get in touch with H. E. Hart and retired Major-General Leslie Beavis who both saw the Red Baron shot down?

Titler agreed to help. With his guidance, I wrote to Hart, Beavis, and other World War I veterans who had seen Richthofen killed. He showed me how to find them by writing to postmasters in the towns where they lived. For retired officers, he advised me to use British and Australian Army veterans' associations.

There is a certain protocol for high-ranking officers, like Major-General Beavis, Malcolm, and your letter would be better received if it is followed.

Most of the veterans answered. I received mail from around the world and showed my friends the exotic stamps from Australia, Germany, England, and Rhodesia, now Zimbabwe. These old soldiers sent photographs of themselves in their army uniforms, drew maps of Richthofen's crash site, and wrote lengthy letters describing what they saw. They in turn suggested other veterans for me to contact. I sent copies of all their notes to Titler.

July 21, 1971
Dear Malcolm,
I'm glad to hear you're having such success with your correspondence on the Richthofen matter and getting such favorable responses. I wonder if you could let me see these items when next you write. I'll return them promptly. Your commitment to research is certainly very gratifying. Warmest regards, Dale M. Titler

I feel humbled now when I consider how these men more than half-way around the world took the time to respond to a boy's curiosity. They were elderly, and some, like Franklyn, in poor health. Yet they put aside whatever they were doing and made time for me, a stranger. My eager questions showed an interest in their lives. I did not understand all that they told me. Their thoughts on the tragedy of battlefield deaths weren't feelings that I could appreciate. War, I thought, was a heroic enterprise. Years later I'd realize how wrong I was.

But I did gain one significant insight: When I asked a question, they answered with a story.

August 7, 1971
Dear Young Friend,
I am sorry that I have not been able to reply to your letter sooner. The fact is I had a heart attack that curtailed my activities for some weeks. It is only now I am beginning to function again with some confidence.
I cannot imagine an Australian boy of thirteen being interested in a German airman, particularly in these times. You must be interested in aeronautics. When I was thirteen, planes were unknown. Indeed, Richthofen's biplane was a crude affair compared to the fighters of today. Children of today have everything. When I was a boy there was no radio. No television and where I lived, no trains. Yet we enjoyed life and the fun we made for ourselves.

I remember how sad I felt when I saw the body of Richthofen. A splendid young man looking handsome and peaceful in death before his time although all those years ago must make him seem old to you. I was twenty-seven then. I am eighty now and know now how young a man he was. Yours, H. E. Hart

The following year, I reached H. D. Billings, a wireless operator mechanic and signalman in Number 3 Squadron, Australian Imperial Force.

February 5, 1972
Dear Malcolm,
I would have to look back fifty-four years to 1918 and not confuse the Red Baron's death with many other incidents that remained fixed in my mind.

His military service had begun in Gallipoli on April 25, 1915, almost three years to the day before the Red Baron died. His letter detailed his service in the Australian Light Horse and the Australian Flying Corps. At the end of his letter, he turned to the Red Baron.

And so we come to the Baron. We picked up [his] remains but our squadron was not otherwise involved (although we buried him) and I am afraid I was not particularly excited, although certainly interested, in the Baron. By that time, I had been on active duty for 2 or 3 years and another crashed plane and a dead pilot did not arouse any of us much.

Hoping that the above may be of interest. Yours truly, H. D. Billings
Billings's letter was followed by one from Jack Nugent, Australian 10th Field Ambulance, 3rd Division.

March 15, 1972
Dear Malcolm,
The War Office sent on your letter to me. I was surprised receiving

mail from the USA. However, I am glad to hear from you and know you are interested in the Red Baron.

Yes, Mal, like many others I saw him shot down when our boy broke with the Baron after him putting bursts of machine gun fire at him all the way down. When very low our boy skipped over a ridge and the Baron must have found he was low and behind our lines. He turned right, banked over his right side and suddenly crashed after being shot at. I saw only the two planes and our boy was lucky to get away.

Well, Mal, I hope you can understand this scrawl. It has taken me back over 50 years. Met many of your boys. I was in an American hospital in Bologne, France for two weeks in 1918. Also, my father migrated from Ireland to America and was a naturalized American before coming to Australia.

I guess you see by the map I've enclosed where Melbourne, my place of residence, is (down south as they say). Australia, a young country, is developing fast. America and England are pouring money in by the millions and taking over many of our industries which is causing some concern in places. However, it's nice to have a few dollars splashed around.

Your letter stamped Chicago took me back some years. The firm I worked for were clock makers. Some 30 years or so ago a chronograph (time clock) was made for a race course in Chicago. It would be outdated now as electronic timing has taken over. I was in art metal work such as church work, etc. With best wishes, Regards & Cheerio, Jack Nugent

As I read and reread these letters, I noticed that no two accounts of Richthofen's death were the same. How could that be? I asked Titler. I faced a dilemma common to all researchers using eyewitness testimony, he told me. He urged me to keep asking question until I found the common threads that stitched the stories together. Notice the details the veterans tell about themselves, he advised, the details that make them individual and distinct from one another.

I followed his suggestion and reached out to more of these old soldiers. D. G. Lewis, the British pilot of the eightieth and last plane Richthofen shot down, wrote to me from Salisbury, Rhodesia (Zimbabwe).

May 5, 1972
My dear Malcolm,
I came across your letter of the 19th of July last year but am uncertain whether or not I replied to it so in case I did not I am writing again.

After being shot down by von Richthofen I had the long journey to the prison camp in Graudenz on the banks of the Vistula River which ran below my prison window. You can find the river in an Atlas but I think the name of Graudenz has been changed.

I spent 9 months there and apart from too little food was treated quite well. I was just over 18 years on my capture and since you are 13 years old you will know how hungry I was all the time but had no pantry to raid as you have.

I used to dream of lovely food at night, roast beef and potatoes, lovely bacon and eggs, chocolate puddings and the rest with the result that my pillow used to be wet with the flow of saliva induced by my imaginary meal. That's all for now. Sincerely, D. G. Lewis

To further help me along, Titler directed me to an administrator at the Australian War Memorial. The administrator suggested I write to the Canberra War Office for the names of all World War I veterans who served in the area where Richthofen died. The War Office led me to Major-General Beavis, H. E. Hart's commanding officer. Beavis viewed Richthofen's body shortly after he died.

July 7, 1972
Dear Malcolm Garcia,
Richthofen's body was brought to the outside of my dugout on my stretcher. The only examination I made was to open the front of his

flying jacket. In the center of his left breast was a jagged hole about three quarters inches by one and one half inches. I did not see any other wounds. I might add that when looking at Richthofen's body I could not but feel very sorry and upset that such a fine looking young man had been killed. Sincerely, L. E. Beavis, retired Major-General.

Rupert Radecki, a soldier in the Fifth Division of the Australian Imperial Force, complained that it had taken the War Office five months to forward my letter to him.

July 14, 1972
Dear Malcolm,
It has taken them all this time for the records office you sent your letter to find me. Not very bright of them you no doubt will agree as they would only have to consult the telephone directory to get a lead.

Well, my young friend, I really saw Baron von Richthofen brought down. He was hit by one bullet which hit him in the lower part of his body and travelled upwards and came out of his chest. This story of the bullet I got from an Australian Air Force grounds man name McCarty who prepared the Red Baron for burial.

Richthofen met his death from a bullet fired by an Australian gunner you can rest assured of that. Had the gunners shooting at Richthofen been more accurate, more than one bullet would have found its mark. To give you some idea how fast the guns fired, I saw a German machine gunner get eleven bullets in his forehead before he toppled over. This was on Passchendaele *Ridge in Belgium.*

I felt Radecki's confidence that antiaircraft fire killed Richthofen. His vivid description of the German soldier on Passchendaele Ridge made an impression. Eleven bullets to the head. I imagined the soldier's face exploding like a tomato. I was glad Richthofen had not died that way. A gruesome death did not meld with my idealized notions of war. I remind myself now that I was just a boy resisting a basic truth about war. It doesn't matter where a bullet strikes or how ghastly the death. Dead is dead.

In addition to my questions about Richthofen, I asked Radecki why the Allies called Germans "Jerries," a mystery that continued to perplex me, but he didn't know any more than Franklyn had.

I have no idea why the Germans were called Jerries. Quite often English soldiers had said to me "Jerrys Coomin (coming) over." They were referring to the German night bombers who made it a habit of visiting us after sundown.

In January last, I was on a South Sea Island cruise and met a lad on the ship, who like you, was interested in the Red Baron. It is refreshing to know that there are some boys in the world interested in past history.

I don't recall, but I think Titler must have suggested I enclose postage money as a courtesy because I sent Radecki ten cents for stamps.

I appreciate you sending the dime for a stamp. As I cannot spend it I will put it with my collection of coins & stamps. I am now 80 but not of the tottering type. I still carry on my occupation of company accountant. Best wishes, Rupert Radecki

On October 21, 1972, I received a letter from Max Sheidig, the only German veteran I'd hear from. He had been a mechanic during the war.

Dear Mr. Garcia,
Today I received your letter about Captain Manfred Baron von Richthofen. It is, of course, many years since he gave his life but I remember him very well because I saw him daily since his squadron was on the same field as ours, his was #11, mine #4. The other two, #6 and #10 were on the other side of the railroad embankment. He was born in 1892 and was killed in action in 1918 however I forgot the exact date but it was in the last part of spring and the first part of summer. I myself

never had the time to worry about him because he never talked to me only to the officers and then he came across the field only whenever he had something to say to them. I was only a corporal and the boss of the machine gun crew and our job was to inspect the planes when they came back from the front and repair the guns when they needed to. That was hardly a place for Richthofen to spend his time after returning from the front. I sure wish I could give you more information about him, but I only saw him that was all. All I know about Richthofen is that he led a fine decent life and lost it in a free for all fight when his squadron was attacked by a bigger force than his own. Respectfully, Max K. Scheidig

Frank Wormald, who had served with H. E. Hart, answered my letter of January 21, 1973, with a curt note that said more about his resentment toward the Germans than it did about Richthofen.

Dear Malcolm,
I got your address off Horrie Hart an old war mate of mine. I can't understand the interest you chaps have in the Baron. He is forgotten in Australia. I think that he was just another bloody German warmonger and it was a pity that his father never cut his throat at birth. He just went for the weak flyers. Regards, Frank Wormald

Decades later, as an embedded reporter with the 82nd Airborne Division in Kandahar in 2003, I listened to many American soldiers speak of Afghans as Wormald had spoken of Germans: They hated them. They hated their languages and customs they didn't understand. Hated the difficulty of distinguishing friend from foe. Hated the random guy in the hills taking potshots. Hated IEDs. Boom, and someone's gone. Tried to remember how they looked alive so they wouldn't dwell on how they looked dead. Fucking kill hajis, the soldiers said. Fucking towel heads. At times, I absorbed their hatred like a virus until I hated too. Hated being scared. Hated being on edge. Hated standing out, an obvious target. Hated being hated. Even later, when we returned to the States, we hated because only our hate made sense.

Nine months after I received Wormald's letter, I heard from Billings again, unprompted. He said he had been thinking of me and had decided to give me something *unique to the collection of Red Baron material you have*: a square piece of red fabric from Richthofen's plane.

September 4, 1973
Malcolm, this is very definitely authentic, and you can have no doubt about saying so. I personally cut it from the plane after it had been brought into our squadron. And it is part of the piece I still have. Take good care of it. It is very rare. Yours, H. D. Billings.

I recall holding the small piece of dark red fabric in my hands. I was too young to fully appreciate what Billings had given to me. How he must have run to the plane and cut the fabric himself. Then, some fifty years later, offering a piece of it to a boy he didn't know, halfway around the world. Simply because I had asked him to share his story. It wasn't just a piece of the plane that was his gift. He had validated my efforts, acknowledged my work.

I did not understand this then. I just knew I had acquired something that none of my friends could match. I might not be an A student, I might have been cut from my junior high school soccer team, but I had a piece of Richthofen's plane.

October 10, 1973
Dear Malcolm,
You've certainly developed a fine file on the Richthofen matter and I commend you for your patience and endurance. I am especially

pleased you have obtained a piece of fabric from the Baron's plane. Congratulations! The people who write to you are certainly at ease in telling you the details of the encounter so apparently you have impressed them with your sincerity and interest. This is highly important in writing to anyone for information and recollections. Warm regards, Dale Titler

* * *

September 22, 2005
Dear Mr. Titler,
Last night on my way back to Gramercy, I heard what sounded like trucks behind me on St. Charles Avenue but I couldn't see them. I pulled over. The trucks stopped and National Guard soldiers approached and asked if I was OK. Instead of using headlights, the driver explained, he drove using night-vision goggles.

"Why?" I said.

"Looters won't know when we come up on them. We own the night."

He let me look through his goggles. The world swam before me in a pale green light.

Tonight is another deep black evening without power. Not even a glow on the horizon. The RV feels cramped with we three reporters hunched over our laptops. I'd spent the day at Judson Baptist Church in Walker, Louisiana, about eighty miles outside New Orleans. The church has been sheltering families made homeless by the storm. Classrooms along a narrow hall were converted into dormitory-style rooms with cots and heaps of donated clothes, baby supplies and toys. For some of the children, the shelter has taken on the characteristics of a playground. They run shouting down the halls, skidding around corners and opening doors to bathrooms and offices.

I met Keith Hall and his wife, Rosezina. As we talked, Rosezina held on to their two sons, five-year-old son Ashton and eighteen-day-old Keith Hall Jr. Rosezina had been pregnant with Keith Jr. when

Katrina hit. She and Hall decided to split up when the water started rising in their house. Rosezina and Ashton went to a friend's house on higher ground while Hall stayed behind and packed clothes. When her friend's house started flooding, Rosezina waded and swam through the floodwaters seeking help. The exertion induced labor. A Coast Guard boat found her struggling in the water and evacuated her to Women's Hospital in Baton Rouge where Keith Jr. was born on August 31. Meanwhile, the baby's father was taken by rescuers to the Houston Astrodome where he called Rosezina's aunt. She gave him the hospital phone number. Keith made his way back to Louisiana by bus after the hospital referred Rosezina to the church.

"Our children are safe. Keith Jr. won't even remember this," Keith said and laughed, looking at the sleeping baby. He reached over with his tattooed arms and stroked the infant's forehead. "You can't stop the will of God. This was not in our hands. I'm a little sad, but we're all living."

After I finished writing the Hall story, I connected to Norman's satellite phone and filed it with my editor. The evening was still early and I felt restless and decided to drive into the French Quarter. There were just a few cars out. I noticed all the stars in the clear sky and listened to the sound of dogs barking as I drove onto I-10.

In the Quarter, Humvees barreled down Bourbon Street, upending bags of garbage heaped and stinking beneath vacant apartments and closed stores. A 9:30 p.m. curfew remained in effect, but judging by the crowded sidewalks few people were paying attention to it. The National Guard seemed not to care, either. They stopped me, I showed my ID and they let me move on.

All the businesses in the Quarter were closed except for a bar and a strip joint, Déjà Vu Showgirls, which may explain why the Guard ignored the curfew as much as civilians. The bar hummed with the noise of generators. I sat beside a woman wearing a blue Salvation Army uniform. A string of yellow Christmas lights hung above us from the ceiling and I was reminded of the Shar-e-Naw neighborhood in northwest Kabul. Vendors used the same kind of lights to illuminate *their stalls, and I could see again the legless beggars reaching out to me and how the lights played across their faces and the shadows cast against the sidewalk and the smell of stagnant sewage in open gutters overwhelming even the shadows.*

I tried calling you again but the line remained dead. I dialed the operator to see if she could get through. She told me she had listings for Dale Titler and Dale Titler Jr. She tried the first number. Nothing. I asked her to try the second one. After a moment, I heard a ring, then voice mail kicked in.

"This is Dale Titler Jr. We can't come to the phone right now."

I left a message.

Everyone in the bar, it seemed, had a cigarette. Smoke walled off the ceiling like a cloudy day. Two men shoved into me as they got up to pose for pictures beside a fallen neon sign of two huge breasts with red lights for nipples. People shouted, trying to speak above the blaring, battery-powered CD player, and then the Salvation Army woman, who had been laughing just moments before, started weeping. She covered her face and then raised her face to the ceiling.

"So many homeless people, I've never seen anything like this," she cried.

A group of her colleagues looked at her. A man beside me said, "What's her problem? We haven't seen anything like this, either!"

He slapped my back and guffawed.

"Let's go across the street, brother," he said and tugged my arm.

More out of curiosity than anything else, I followed him and some of his companions into Déjà Vu. Members of the Guard sat at small round tables, their green uniforms spotted with white dots from a mirrored disco ball twirling from the ceiling. Several generators hummed. I watched a gal with tattoos snaking down both her arms stomp onstage in black platform shoes. The Guard guys whooped. One man offered her five dollars. She balled the money into her hand, sat on the edge of the stage and wrapped her legs around his neck.

"I can't believe what I'm doing here. I'm a Cub Scout master at home," the man yelled to no one.

Then a Red Cross volunteer jumped onstage, tore off her T-shirt and wiggled out of her pants. Everyone's mouth dropped. The stripper stared at her, shrugged and then yielded the stage. Kneeling before a table of National Guard, the volunteer leaned down and buried her face in a soldier's lap. His eyes could not have gotten any wider, the guys with him hooting with laughter. She raised her head and leered at them. Then she paused as if something horrid had occurred to her, and her expression veered between desperation and terror. She stood up, covered her crotch and shouted in an alarmed voice, "Get away from me, get away from me, everyone get away from me!"

"I gotta get a picture of this," the scoutmaster said.

"No!" the stripper shouted. "No pictures! No pictures! You don't do that to her!"

She demanded to see the camera to be sure he had deleted the photo. Then she stepped around the sobbing volunteer and stalked offstage. Another stripper worked tables, flirting with the Guard, oblivious of all the commotion. She played with the hair of one acne-scarred young soldier and I watched him melt before her as she reached for his wallet. The volunteer emerged from the crowd and sat at a table near me.

"You don't think bad of me, do you?" she asked a man beside her.

"No," he said.

He put an arm around her, then noticed I was watching.

"Were you in Vietnam, Jerry?"

"Jerry?"

"Jerry Garcia, dude. You look just like him."

"It's the beard and ponytail."

"Duh."

"No, I was too young for Vietnam."

"Wish I could say the same."

"You were in Vietnam?"

"Dude, if you were too young for Vietnam, I wasn't even born yet. Iraq, man. I was in Iraq."

"Understood," I said.

I went outside, pushing past a group of teenage boys peering inside Déjà Vu. Across the street, two cops were squaring off with each other. One of them landed some impressive punches. I asked the boys what was going on. They glanced at the cops, shrugged, and turned their attention back to the strippers. My cell phone rang and I answered.

"Hello?"

"Hello. This is Dale Titler Jr."

* * *

Throughout junior high and high school, I stayed in touch with H. E. Hart and Rupert Radecki. Radecki retired about a year after I first heard from him. He and his wife took cruises in the South Pacific, visiting New Caledonia, the New Hebrides, Fiji, Tonga, and New Zealand, among other places I'd not heard of. *If ever you visit the North Island of New Zealand,* he wrote in 1972, *take a trip down to Rotorua to see the geysers and boiling mud and steam coming up from the ground in numerous places. I thought Australia had a lot of sheep. New Zealand has sixty million head of sheep and some of the finest cattle I have ever seen. At present we are having a vicious thunderstorm with very bright flashes of lightning.*

I enjoyed his letters but I did not respond as quickly as I once had. The Vietnam War was winding down and with it the allure of becoming a fighter pilot. Memories of my fantasy squadron, the Bald Eagles, made me burn with embarrassment.

No longer enthralled by Richthofen, I sought new research projects, new heroes. Inspired by the movie *Butch Cassidy and the Sundance Kid,* I began studying outlaws of the American West. I wrote to Robert Redford, who'd starred as the Sundance Kid, for information about Cassidy and his Wild Bunch gang. Redford sent me an autographed photo. In a separate letter, his secretary put me in touch with Cassidy's sister, Lula Betenson, then in her nineties. Betenson told me she believed her brother did not die in Bolivia as depicted in the film but returned to the United States and spent the remaining years of his life in Washington.

March 15, 1974
Dear Malcolm,
You've done very, very well on the Butch Cassidy research. I'm proud of you for your obvious professional work on digging out the material firsthand such as the Betenson interview. You must think seriously about writing accounts or even books about your subjects. All best wishes, Dale M. Titler.

Titler apologized for not responding to my letter as soon as he would have liked. He had suffered a bout with pneumonia that had left him bedridden for weeks. Almost a year later, ill health and age caught up with H. E. Hart.

January 6, 1975
Dear Mr. Garcia,
First let me wish you every happiness this new year. Your card to my husband H. E. Hart arrived in time for Christmas but I thought I would let the joyous season pass before I told you my sad news. My husband died on the 29th of August. He was a remarkable man. Keen intellect and active. He enjoyed corresponding with you and admired your interest. Really, he wasted a great talent. He had a marvelous grip of English and had a flair for writing. He never mentioned it but he was decorated for bravery in the field on the 8th August, 1918. Many Americans were in the same breakthrough of the German lines and suffered heavy casualties. That offensive really ended the 1914–1918 war.
Best wishes for your new study of the American outlaw—there seems to be plenty of them about in these days all over the world. Yours sincerely, (Mrs.) C. Veronica Hart

When I wasn't reading about Butch Cassidy, I'd catch the "L" train into Chicago with my friend Tom, rattling along the worn, rusted tracks until we got off on the skid row of South Michigan Avenue. We hung out in dimly lit bars thick with cigarette smoke that didn't bother to card us—a couple of kids, rebels with a curfew. We saw old women wearing wigs stiff as straw, and men whose sad eyes, missing teeth, and faded tattoos said more about their lives than words could have. They teased the rims of their glasses with tobacco-stained fingers and spoke in hoarse tones as they hustled us for change. One man showed me the mottled real estate business cards he still kept in his wallet.

I remember a red-haired woman named Carol. Her dirt-streaked face looked to me as wrinkled as a rumpled shirt. Her clothes reeked of cigarettes. She told me she made forty dollars a day, an enormous sum to me. How? I wanted to know.

"Honey," she said, "I beg."

When I got home, I didn't dare tell my parents where Tom and I had been. Instead, I kept a diary. I began with one sentence, *I was in a bar tonight*, and took it from there. *Honey, I beg.* I wrote it down, afraid somehow that if I didn't I'd forget the choice expressions and individual stories. I had no idea what I'd do with my diary any more than I knew what I'd do with the Richthofen and Butch Cassidy material. I just knew it was worth keeping.

In 1975, Saigon fell to the communists in a renewed offensive. I overheard my parents in the kitchen criticize President Ford for not aiding an ally. "If Nixon were still president . . ." they said, still stunned by Watergate.

Politics and foreign policy mattered little to me. As helicopters swept terrified Americans from the rooftop of the US Embassy in Saigon, I was preparing to graduate from high school and enroll at Ripon College in Wisconsin in the fall. I'd also begun dating my first girlfriend. Julie was shy but smart, plain but adventurous. I thought I loved her and worried I would lose her to someone else.

She gave me a clothbound copy of *The Day the Red Baron Died* for my birthday. It had long been out of print. Because it was a surprise, she would not tell me where she had found it.

July 23, 1975
Dear Malcolm,
I am pleased that your girl and you have a common interest in the Red Baron. I sometimes get letters from the female sex on the subject of the German ace; apparently they find him "irresistible." But hang in there. Maybe some of his charm will rub off. I keep hoping it will in my case, anyway.

As always, Titler wished me well. Normally, he signed his full name. This time, however, he wrote *Dale*. I continued to call him Mr. Titler out of respect.

* * *

September 24, 2005
Dear Mr. Titler,
It was a pleasure speaking to your wife, Helen, last night after getting your cell number from your son, Dale Jr. Sorry you were out when I called. As I told Helen, I will drive to Gulfport when I finish my work in New Orleans. I hope that will be soon. I hear the roads to Mississippi will open any day now.
*   Small signs of life have begun popping up in New Orleans. Some families, for instance, have been allowed into Chalmette, in St. Bernard Parish where I was today on Victor Street and Bonita Drive. Filmy water lines wrapped around houses just below second-floor windows. The humid air had an odor of rot that I could almost taste at the back of my throat. Light mixed with shadows in the branches of trees. Cell phones rang. Families in rubber boots and hip waders trudged in and*

out of their homes carrying buckets of mud they dumped on their lawns adding to the stink, and the sun burned in a clear sky and the whole neighborhood steamed in the heat.

One woman, Dora Williams on Bonita Drive, her face streaked with dirt, showed me a teacup she had salvaged from her home. She rinsed it off with a bottle of water. Dancing Asian characters emerged from the dirty runoff. Through the open door of her house, I saw a closet door open, a tongue of mud oozing out.

"How is it this wasn't broken?" she wondered about the cup.

A National Guard jeep pulled up in front of her house. The driver asked us if we needed help.

"No, thank you," Williams said.

"There's a lot of looting going on. Gangs too," the soldier said.

"Nothing here," Williams said.

"How about FEMA? The Red Cross? Have you heard from them?"

"No," she said.

Pop, pop, I heard from about a block away. Pop, pop. The National Guard soldier cocked his head toward the sound and without another word got in his jeep and raced away.

Williams looked at me. "Gunshots?" she said.

A helicopter flew overhead, then veered away.

The National Guard soldier returned minutes later. It was nothing, he told us. Aerosol cans exploding in a garage from the heat. He wished us a good day and left again. I thanked Williams for her time and got back into my SUV.

Before I returned to Gramercy, I drove to West Jefferson Medical Center in Marrero. The hospital had no air-conditioning for four days after Katrina. Temperatures reached 100 degrees and higher inside. Generators powered fans, but that did little to relieve the heat. Doctors and nurses cut the legs and sleeves off their scrubs to stay cool. Elderly patients suffered. Nurses could not bathe them or provide them with as much water as they wanted. At the same time, people were coming in for help. One woman brought in an hours-old infant she had delivered herself in the attic of her flooded house. Another woman was thirty-seven weeks pregnant and unable to reach her regular physician.

"We were rolling here without air-conditioning and running water, but we never lost our ability to operate," surgeon Craig Thompson told me.

Within twenty-four hours after Katrina had passed, doctors saw one man who had been stabbed in an evacuation shelter, a police officer shot in the head, two alleged looters shot in the chest, a family of four shot and a man injured after he crashed into a Humvee. One pregnant patient said she was past her due date. After the baby was delivered, a boy, doctors realized he was about four weeks premature.

"Katrina was different than anything that has come through here," Thompson told me. He had lost his house and lived at the hospital. Until recently he used a boat to visit his flooded house. Of the 450 medical staff members, only 150 have returned to work. Some, like Thompson, lived at the hospital now because they had no other place to go.

When I finished talking to Thompson, I drove back to Gramercy to write the day's stories. I flipped on the AC in the SUV and turned on the radio. A DJ came on and said a second storm was approaching the Gulf Coast. It already had a name, Hurricane Rita.

* * *

At Ripon College, the research projects I had engaged in when I was younger never translated into scholastic excellence. My parents let me know in no uncertain terms that they expected more from me than a low C average. I didn't know what to say. College seemed to be nothing more than an extension of high school. Little inspired my interest. I grew tired of taking one meaningless course after another. I skipped most of my classes but not theater. My mother's brother, Joe, was an actor. Influenced by his appearances in movies and on TV, I auditioned for the drama department's production of the Terrence McNally comedy *Bad Habits.* I got the part of a sanitarium patient. Acting soon garnered my passion. On stage I was no longer a directionless student but an utterly different character divorced from my life and surroundings by the imagination of a playwright. After the final curtain, however, the drudgery of my classes resumed.

April 14, 1977
Dear Malcolm: I'm pleased to hear how serious you are about theater. So many people are content to just get along and take things as they come today. Believe me when I say your dedication to a job well done will pay off later in life. Warm regards, Dale

At the end of my sophomore year, bored and restless, full of a false confidence that came from having lived on my own for almost two years, I transferred to Coe College in Cedar Rapids, Iowa, where I had friends from high school. I majored in English and theater.

June 8, 1977
Dear Malcolm: Very nice to hear from you again and be brought up to date on your latest activities. Keep up the good work and don't be upset by raised eyebrows and the loss of administration friendship [at Ripon College]. It's people like you who change the world for the better. Best of luck in your new college. Yours, Dale

My love for the theater and Titler's confidence in my future did nothing to alleviate my parents' concern. Neither did my 2.0 grade-point average when I graduated from Coe in May 1979. Adrift, I moved to New York City in September to pursue acting. Manhattan was also where Uncle Joe lived. I rented an apartment in a condemned Brooklyn brownstone on Cumberland Street, one floor above an alcoholic who collected stray cats and allowed them to use his bathtub as a litter pan. In the winter, the stench of cat pee rose through my noisy radiators, making my room nearly intolerable. Joe and his wife, Stella, often invited me to dinner, reassuring my mother that I wasn't starving.

I recall sitting with Joe in his 57th Street apartment as he listened to recordings of interviews he had given and critiqued his voice. He noticed when he mumbled, spoke in a monotone, and when his comments lacked precision. He encouraged me to pause between words when I didn't know how to continue a thought rather than fill the silence with um, uh, or er. I liked his deep, rich voice, its sense of purpose and authority, and I followed his advice. Before I spoke I began considering what I would say and how I would say it rather than spouting the first unformed thought that came into my head. I was a college graduate, legally an adult, but I didn't feel like one. I had no idea what I wanted to do, but I wanted to speak in a way that sounded as if I did.

January 30, 1980
Dear Malcolm,
Nice indeed to hear from you again and hear of your new experiences in the big city. The only time I was ever in NYC was at a stopover in LaGuardia. Never really had the urge to live there—it's safer not to, I think. It's dog eat dog, but if you can survive a year of it, the addition to your writing repertoire will be well worth while.

Perhaps I didn't tell you earlier, but I was promoted to Kessler Historian in May a year ago and enjoy the work very much. It cuts into my freelance writing time, but I still find time to write on the side. Dodd, Mead has asked me to rewrite my first book, Wings of Mystery, *for them so they can put it out in a new edition, and I'll be busy on that beginning in mid-July.*

I enjoyed your letter and it was good to know you're still in there working hard. Don't get discouraged, keep plugging away and sooner or later you'll get the right break. Warmest regards, Dale.

My theater auditions never resulted in a director casting me in a play. Instead of earning a living as an actor, I accepted jobs through day labor joints in New York and across the country. I answered phones for the University of New York, filed grant applications for a YMCA on Wall Street, operated a paper shredder, and worked as a hospital receptionist at Sloan Kettering.

When I got tired of New York, I trained as a whitewater rafting guide in Idaho and then cleaned test tubes for a Minneapolis lab. I rented rooms in houses that whistled with wind blowing through cracks in the walls, and I took in stray cats for company. I met construction workers, waitresses, Vietnam combat veterans, stock clerks, accountants, drunks, prostitutes, and junkies, and wherever I found them, I asked questions.

About living, they'd tell me: "Have a good rest of your life"; about traveling: "All it takes is a thumb and some guts"; about a good car: "It's as clean as it wanna be." A tall, attractive woman was "fine." They said "man" and at other times "m*aaa*n!"

The stories I heard about hitchhiking, fistfights, job loss, and war were told in ways that made my feet ache from miles I'd never walked, my head pound from problems I didn't have, my heart sink from losses I'd never experienced.

I wrote it all down and continued my nomadic existence. My parents never knew where I'd be from one week to the next. I called home every Saturday. On occasion, when I had a somewhat permanent address, I'd write a letter. My mother responded to these short notes with enthusiasm, encouraging me to write more. *You know a phone call is great*, she wrote, *but there is something about a letter. Thoughts on paper, not fleeting words airborne, is much more satisfying.*

I could hear the disappointment in my father's voice about the life I was living, but Uncle Joe approved of my wandering. Or, I should say, he didn't disapprove of it. He told me I reminded him of his own mother, who left for parts unknown for weeks at a time when she quarreled with my grandfather and was dubbed an "eccentric" traveler by her family.

One March morning in 1980, a man sat next to me in a Minneapolis bagel shop on Lake Street. He ordered coffee and we began talking. He said he'd been hopping freight trains across the country. Just got off one, in fact. I asked him how he did it. You go to a "division point," he explained, a rail yard where trains traveling across the country stop to load and unload. Determine which direction the trains are going, and just get on one.

Division point. Something about the phrase appealed to me. I finished my bagel, walked back to my room, and wrote a story about a guy who had jumped freights when he was young but was now stuck in a dead-end job with coworkers who had never traveled beyond their commute to and from work.

More fiction followed. I wrote about a homeless woman in New York taking comfort in a stray cat. In another story a man and a woman meet in a diner. He doesn't have the money to pay for their meal. The woman walks out when she realizes the big plans the man has for finding a job are nothing more than fantasy.

I submitted these and other stories to college magazines. Editors rejected them with form letters, but I kept writing.

October 27, 1980
Dear Malcolm,
Not to throw a damper on your efforts, but I have given up writing. It's just too much bother to fight with publishers by long distance and the rank and file of publishers aren't, by any means, an honest lot. I say this after six books and half a hundred articles in periodicals. It's just not worth it any more, Malcolm. Enjoyed your short stories you sent me;

I think you're off to a fine start. Every good wish as always. Excuse the brevity of my note, please. Warmest regards, Dale.

In the summer of 1982, I enrolled in the creative writing program at the University of Missouri in Columbia. I also submitted stories to the *Columbia Daily Tribune* with little success.

August 17, 1982
Dear Malcolm,
I must agree with your observation about interviewing people; the best way is to see them face-to-face. However, I use the telephone a lot, especially on weekends when the rates are low. Once you contact a person you want to interview, ask them if you can send them a list of questions (number them) and telephone them at a certain time to discuss them. Use a tape recorder on the phone to record both sides of the conversation. Then transcribe the tape and use it as research material. Hang in there, Malcolm. You'll make it yet. Sincerely, Dale

A young woman I met at a party and fell blindingly in love with proved a significant distraction, however. Linda had long brown hair and a sway to her walk as if nothing else mattered. She also was as far from being monogamous as the moon is from the earth. In my heartbreak, I missed classes and flunked out of my second semester.

I left Missouri for San Francisco in May 1983 for no other reason than that a childhood friend, Gabrielle, lived in North Beach and needed a roommate. Her apartment at the top of Vallejo Street overlooked the bay, and I'd often stare at the water and the Bay Bridge and think how far away I was from Winnetka.

I had not been in San Francisco long when I began volunteering at the Ozanam Center on Howard Street south of Market. The center, a program of the St. Vincent de Paul Society, was named after a sixteenth-century French social worker. It offered a twenty-four-hour alcohol detox unit on the second floor of a brick building that from the outside reminded me of a warehouse. The first floor, called the drop-in center, served as a place for homeless people to spend the day reading, sleeping, or playing cards. At night, staff and volunteers converted the drop-in to a night shelter capable of handling up to fifty men. Women in need of shelter were referred elsewhere.

I had crossed paths with dozens of homeless people in the years I spent traveling the country and thought the center would be a good way to fill my time while I looked for work. I had not been volunteering long before Gabrielle put me out of her apartment because her boyfriend was jealous. She suggested that I apply for welfare. Instead I stayed at the center, hoarding what little I earned through temp jobs. For weeks, I listened to men thrash around in their sleep, scream in the middle of the night and wake up from their nightmares wild–eyed and exhausted.

"What did you dream?" I would ask.

One Vietnam veteran we all called Red because of his thick red beard told me he had nightmares about the people he had killed. "Another enemy dead in Vietnam today," he said when he woke up. "I got 'em in my sleep." He didn't remember any good days from when he was in the army. "There weren't too many over there," he said.

I wrote it down.

I thought I'd live for a few months in San Francisco and then leave for another city, another state, as I'd done before. This time, however, I stayed. I didn't think much of my temp jobs, but I enjoyed my work at the Ozanam Center, the characters I met who, like Red, knew one another by their street names: Too Tall, a homeless man who was seven feet; Alabama, a southerner with a patchy red beard who suffered alcoholic seizures; Rocky, a guy who had a loopy, aw-shucks grin, among many others. They taught me pinochle, chess, and dominoes. They borrowed a dollar here, a dollar there, money I knew I'd never see again. I was twenty-five and still had zits. They called me kid.

As the kid, I was assigned the grunt jobs: cleaning bathrooms, picking up trash outside, and working behind the coffee counter with Lyle, another volunteer. Lyle liked to wear white button-down shirts and creased gray slacks. He was fortysomething, balding, stooped, and had a slight paunch. I could imagine him standing by my father on a platform, waiting to catch a train into Chicago. He had been an accountant in "a previous life," he told me. He carried a leather briefcase and made a great display of removing file folders from it as if he still had clients. At the time, Lyle had been sober two months.

Then he stopped showing up. I assumed he'd quit, until one afternoon when I saw one of the shelter staff help him through the door. His clothes were torn and covered with dried mud. Cuts and bruises scarred his unshaven face. One eye was swollen shut. His hands shook as he sat down.

"Where have you been staying?" a counselor known as Gypsy asked him.

"Outside. Golden Gate Park," Lyle said.

I looked at Lyle. He returned my look, then turned away. Gypsy leafed through a thick worn file with a flap reading *Norton, Lyle*. Inserting a blank page, he asked Lyle how long he had been drinking this time.

In August 1983, the Ozanam Center hired me as an intake worker for its detox program. At first, I worked the overnight shift. Then, after two months, I was moved to days. I signed homeless men and women into detox and put their names on waiting lists for inpatient alcohol programs. They were expected to stay sober while they waited for an opening. Sometimes six weeks passed before a program had a bed available. By then, most of my clients had been in and out of detox several times and were no longer considered eligible.

Those who managed to hang tough were rejected too, victims of their own white-knuckle discipline. If they could last six weeks without drinking, a Salvation Army social worker told me, they didn't need to be in a program. I would soon learn that rejection is part of an alcoholic's life, the elixir of addiction. The guys who were refused took the news calmly. They asked me for BART money. I knew they weren't going to buy a BART ticket, but I gave them the money anyway. I wasn't going to hold them accountable for the failings of some by-the-book jerk on the other end of a phone who had the power to deny an alcoholic the help he or she needed. I watched guys who had fought against their desire to drink for weeks leave to buy a bottle of Thunderbird or Night Train.

"Sorry, Malcolm," they would tell me on their way out the door.

I saved my money and found an apartment on Masonic Street in Haight-Ashbury. I wrote fiction at night and continued to receive form-letter rejections. The enjoyment I experienced in my job balanced the disappointment. In 1984, I enrolled in the Graduate School of Social Work at San Francisco State University to ensure a future in social services. I also took a creative writing class.

At work I noticed that many of the homeless people we admitted to detox liked to write poetry and draw. In 1987, with the help of a colleague, I put together an anthology of their writings and illustrations. We called it *Out of the Rain*. Then we started a monthly publication, *By No* **MEANS**. The name came from a lyric in the song "King of the Road": *I'm a man of means by no means / king of the road. By No* **MEANS** carried stories written by the homeless about life on the street. Those who couldn't write, we interviewed. I followed the advice Titler had given me while I was in Columbia about using a recorder.

November 7, 1991
Dear Malcolm,
So there you are! I've thought of you many times and have wondered how you fared in the world. Now I see you've done well—with your

own newspaper! Not bad going at all. I'm proud of you. My best,
Dale

Titler had been keeping busy himself. He was researching a book about the death of Glenn Miller, the bandleader whose plane disappeared over the English Channel in 1944. He had also begun writing screenplays. His three children were grown and he was a grandparent of a two-year-old boy. His wife had retired but continued to work part-time at a school. *All of those who helped me so generously with my book on von Richthofen have passed away,* he wrote, *and I'm not even in touch with their survivors anymore. Time moves on. I hope they are not forgotten.*

In September 1987, I left the Ozanam Center to direct the Tenderloin Self-Help Center, an agency for homeless mentally ill people, including veterans suffering post-traumatic stress disorder. Despite my excitement about my new job, I felt tired. The bohemian call of social work, the finger snapping, hey-man-I'm-living-on-the-edge rap had lost its allure. The daily numbing of my heart as I dealt with the same people over and over again drained me.

Only one percent of the more than one hundred men and women who daily came through our doors entered substance-abuse programs. We had no statistics on how many actually completed them. Those of our clients who found jobs signed up for shelter because their minimum wage-salaries couldn't cover rent even for a welfare hotel room. But they were working and thus weren't eligible for shelter. They had money, therefore should have been able to find someplace to stay. That was the thinking, a rationalization for triage. We didn't have enough room to shelter everybody.

If they drank, however, they could get into detox. Income didn't matter if you were drunk. Many tried controlled drinking—just enough to get into detox, have a roof over their head for the night so they could work the next morning. They were back on the street in no time.

I could have scolded them with patronizing nonsense to show my moral superiority but I wasn't in a position to judge. I grew up in a ritzy Chicago suburb where alcoholics weren't drunks but neighbors and acquaintances who'd had a little too much to drink on a Friday night. Somehow they managed to stumble out of bed the next day. Somehow their families covered for them. Somehow their despair found a parachute.

We had no parachutes at the Ozanam Center. At best, we offered homeless people a safe place to spend their days and nights as they slowly killed themselves. We held memorial services under highway overpasses where they had died, to honor them and let God know they were worth remembering. Traffic rushed by as we stepped around discarded fast food wrappers and pop cans. Some prayed. Others of us just closed our eyes so that those who prayed thought we believed in a higher power too. I felt the empty space in the crowd at the center's front door when a regular was gone.

Another kind of space opened when I visited home.

"Oh, social services," friends of my family would say with a long, lingering pause when I told them about my job. They were the kind of people who praised those who helped others, but had a poor opinion of those in need. They considered charitable work an activity of the church, worthy of a dollar donation on Sundays, not a career for their children. They shot dismayed looks at my parents, but maintained their forced smiles.

"That must be very rewarding," they'd say before changing the subject.

During my seven years at the Self-Help Center, state budget cuts in social programs added to my funk. I laid off staff. In 1993, I had to let go of Roberta Murray, who helped at the front desk. Formerly homeless, she would sign in people for appointments with our benefits advocate. She said nothing when I told her I'd eliminated her position. She did not seem particularly disturbed. You're eligible for unemployment, I told her. She said she understood. She didn't. Or she did and knew that despite my assurances, she would be doing without. After all, she had been homeless before. In the end, I'll never know what she thought. I kept my program operating in part by eliminating her $16,000-a-year salary. Roberta returned to her Eddy Street apartment that night, overdosed on prescription medication, and died.

Friends told me I was not responsible for her death. Maybe, but by then I'd had it. Although the state of California could continue ruining lives with its budget cuts, I didn't have to be its executioner. I resigned in 1994.

That year I also self-published a book of short stories, *Division Point*. Most of the characters were based on the people I'd met in San Francisco and earlier when I was temping across the country, people who had taken a wrong turn and were headed for a train wreck. I sent copies of *Division Point* to my family. My father was not impressed and threw his copy away unread. Self-publishing, he said, suggested that no one thought much of my work. He had a point. The stories had all been rejected by magazine editors.

My mother, however, buoyed me. In response to *Division Point*, she sent me a 1927 anthology of Henry Wadsworth Longfellow's poetry. The leather-bound volume barely held together, its pages dry and flimsy, the binding cracked and peeling. In a note she enclosed, my mother wrote that Longfellow was her favorite poet as a child. She wanted me, *my writer son*, to have it *for the inspiration*.

February 26, 1994
Dear Malcolm,
Congratulations on your first book! I want to see you go on and do more books and receive distribution through a commercial publisher. Keep going; you can do it. I had a triple bypass last November, and am just getting over that. At 68, one doesn't bounce back as quickly. All the best, Dale

I was done with helping the homeless but not with writing. I used my experience publishing *By No* **MEANS** to get freelance journalism gigs, and, in 1995, I enrolled in the Graduate School of Journalism at the University of California–Berkeley. Two years later, I graduated and accepted an internship at the *Philadelphia Inquirer* that led to a job at the *Kansas City Star* in November 1998.

I wrote to Titler from Philadelphia and Kansas City but he never responded. After his 1994 letter, I stopped hearing from him. I thought he might just not be feeling well, or perhaps my letters to him had been lost in the mail. It was nothing, I told myself. He's just busy. At times I considered driving to Gulfport and meeting him. After all, we had been corresponding for more than twenty years.

I never followed through, however, afraid our relationship would somehow suffer if we met. What if we had nothing to say to each other? What if we didn't even like each other? After all, I wasn't a thirteen-year-old boy romanticizing a dead fighter pilot anymore. The thought of possibly spoiling what had been a wonderful pen-pal relationship by a face-to-face meeting completely unnerved me. Yet I continued writing to him, always hoping for a response, a throwback to the days when I was much younger and the thought that someone who had written a book would bother writing to me made the world feel alive and full of possibilities.

In Kansas City I worked the night cops beat. I covered shootings, and waited in bleak neighborhoods behind strips of yellow police tape while cops walked through a house where someone had been killed or examined a car in which a body had been discovered. People would gather on the street and ask me, "What's going on?" I answered with what I knew, and they told me their stories. What it was like to live on a street where drive-by shootings were a common occurrence. How it felt to lose a son or daughter to murder and find yourself raising your grandchildren. How they felt safer in a bus shelter than they did in their own homes.

I listened, asked questions, took notes. More often than not, editors at the *Star* were uninterested in these interviews. Nice color, they said. Good for a quote or two. I thought they were worth more. After work I took my notes and wrote about lives lived beneath the news radar and submitted them to small magazines. Unlike my fiction, these pieces were picked up. I kept at it.

Nearly three years after I started at the *Star*, terrorists attacked New York and Washington, D.C., on September 11, 2001. That evening I asked the assistant managing editor, Randy Smith, to send me to Afghanistan. I was forty-three. If I was going to have a breakout moment as a reporter, 9/11 was it. Smith, however, was noncommittal. I wasn't surprised. I assumed that other, far more experienced reporters would get the assignment. Still, I tried, I consoled myself.

Three days before Thanksgiving, Smith called me into the office of the editor, Mark Zieman. Zieman asked me to close the door. As I sat down he peered at me over his glasses from behind his desk.

"You're going to Afghanistan," Zieman said. "Tomorrow."

Stunned, I said nothing.

I could barely get through the rest of the day, overjoyed and scared, my emotions swinging wildly between the two states. I had no knowledge of Afghanistan. I barely knew where it was. I went to Google, typed, "Afghanistan history," and began reading in a panic. After work I bought a journal to keep a diary of the trip.

That night I packed. Then I lay in bed and stared at the ceiling, wondering what I had gotten myself into. Be careful what you wish for, you might get it. I don't know where I'd heard that expression but it seemed appropriate now.

The next morning Smith drove me to the airport. I flew to Washington, then Vienna, then New Delhi and Islamabad, where I caught a United Nations flight to Kabul. I arrived in Afghanistan on November 28, 2001 woozy with jet lag. The next night, I began writing in my journal. To help me focus, I decided to address my entries to friends, Titler the first among them.

November 29, 2001
Dear Mr. Titler,
I flew into Kabul yesterday. This city's shot to hell. Rubble everywhere. Collapsed buildings. Abandoned Soviet tanks from the time of the Russian invasion line either side of the roads leading into the city. I recall scenes of World War I described in your book. You spoke of a wall that spilled into a street. All the ruined and demolished houses, the blown tree trunks. That's Kabul. I equate the city with the Tenderloin in San Francisco. The boarded-up buildings. The abandoned cars. The lost look on people's faces. The begging. This is one big poor neighborhood. Very different to be sure from my days in social services, but still a point of comparison I use to make Kabul feel less foreign, the war less threatening.

December 15, 2001
Dear Mr. Titler,
Another day in Kabul. There's no central heating. It's freezing and the concrete buildings here hold the cold, making it feel even colder. Everyone has space heaters but there's no power so the space heaters don't work. We sit by them anyway for the idea of heat we imagine them producing.
I've made the rounds of key ministries part of my daily schedule. Interior, foreign affairs, defense. San Francisco had a slew of deputy mayors, one for what seemed like every activity in the city. I remember how I'd meet with them pleading for funding. Now I plead with ministers for information. Same difference. Red tape is red tape no matter what part of the world you're in.

December 21, 2001
Dear Mr. Titler,
Tonight I was out after curfew. My driver, Khalid, and I were held for six hours at a military checkpoint in south Kabul. We had

attended an evening news conference an hour away at Bagram Air Base where American forces are stationed. On the way back, our car had a flat. We didn't have a spare. We drove for two hours on the rim in first gear. When we reached a downtown checkpoint, a Northern Alliance soldier raised his rifle and aimed at the windshield. Three other soldiers joined him. The first soldier told us he would hold us until 5 a.m., when curfew ended. He asked for a cigarette and I gave him one. He looked at the tire and said we shouldn't have been driving on a flat.

January 28, 2002
Dear Mr. Titler,
Outside Kabul today, I saw rogue militias set up roadblocks that my driver and I paid bribes to get through. On the Jalalabad Road, American military patrols roared past us with .50-caliber guns, and women covered in body-length veils turned away from the spewing dust. Farther beyond the capital, I watched Northern Alliance soldiers barter their weapons in a market bazaar in Tokhchy village, only minutes from Bagram Air Base. Crowds mobbed the dusty clay street bartering for spices, clothes and fabric. Three rocket-propelled grenades were strapped to a motorcycle outside Rahim Tea Shop. Northern Alliance soldiers displayed their weapons inside. I wrote about one young man, Said Akeer, who offered to sell me his Kalashnikov. He said he'd been fighting since he was fourteen. First the Russians and then the civil war that followed their withdrawal, and then the Taliban.

When I turned down the rifle, he offered to sell me a Taliban prisoner for $1,000. I told him no. He opened his coat and displayed two pistols. Again I said no.

"I'm not fighting now that the Taliban are gone," Akeer said. "I have to make money."

February 3, 2002
Dear Mr. Titler,
No power this evening. I use a car battery to operate my laptop. Gunfire somewhere in the city. Everyone has a gun in Kabul. So many guns I no longer notice. There was a chapter in your book where you described the Red Baron as tired. He'd look out at the muddy airfield of wherever he was stationed and just felt beat. I've not seen combat yet, but I've seen what wars leave behind. I know what it's like to wake up and look at all the cratered buildings here and all the homeless and all the war wounded and all the infants held by widows. There is a heaviness to destruction and need that wears me down. I felt that in San Francisco, where I could help people. I feel it more here where I cannot.

I think that parts of Kabul resemble photographs I've seen of London after the Nazi blitz. My parents spoke of WWII as I speak of Vietnam now. I remember them recalling newsreels of destroyed cities. How shocked they were at the destruction. It didn't seem real, so outside the realm of where they were. It's very real here.

At sunset when all the rubble is darkened by shadows and the sky-line is red-hued, Kabul can be really beautiful. Such a contrast to the daytime when all I see are people who lost legs and arms to mines begging in the streets. How they mob me, pleading, and I remember homeless people in San Francisco collecting around me like that but never with such intensity, and they weren't armless and legless and they weren't holding children who look at me with the eyes of puppies.

I left Afghanistan for Kansas City at the end of March 2002. My editors gave me some time off. I took long walks through my west side neighborhood, trying to wrap my head around being back. Sometimes I ventured downtown, but only early in the morning when few people were about so I wouldn't feel squeezed and hemmed in. In place of maimed men and women, I saw families arguing about which eighty-dollar sneakers to buy in malls. Instead of mud huts nestled up against barren foothills, skyscrapers blotted out the sun. Instead of Afghan police swinging metal chains to disperse crowds, I watched police officers issue parking tickets beneath a billboard of a nearly nude model promoting a brand of booze.

I summarized my journal entries and my feelings of dislocation in a letter to Titler, but still he didn't respond. I thought he must have died. After all, he had been sick and was getting on in years. However, I never really believed it. I'd always assumed one more letter from me would prompt a response. That he was still in Gulfport. That he was just older, slower. That he was still there with an encouraging word, bolstering me with his confidence.

* * *

September 25, 2005
Dear Mr. Titler,
Hurricane Rita struck western Louisiana last night. Before the storm, I wrote a feature about Johnny White's Sports Bar, a dive in the French Quarter whose claim to fame is that it stayed open during Katrina. Despite Rita, the regulars were planning a pub crawl through the Quarter. Crazy, I know. They even had army cots for people to sleep off their drunk.

I was alone in the RV when Rita came through. Norm and the other reporter had returned home days earlier. Headlong slants of rain came down in torrents. The RV swayed, and I felt it lift off the ground, and I pressed my hands against the walls for balance. The door snapped open to a howling wind and the air vibrated and trembled. Ink-black clouds convulsed against an even blacker sky, and the cries of the wind turned to screams as tree branches snapped and slammed against the RV. I thought at times that it might tip over.

In the morning, I woke up to a gray sky blocking the sun. No birds, no squirrels. Rain pelted the RV and thunder boomed inter-mittently, rumbling through a whip-snapping wind. I contacted my editor for the day's assignment, my last story. I'm to leave tomorrow for

Kansas City. He told me to drive to Lake Charles Civic Center, west of New Orleans, where families were seeking refuge. The drive there was treacherous. Rain drenched the interstate. Passing military trucks swamped my SUV, and for seconds I was submerged. Drivers in military convoys blasted their horns as they passed me, and I swerved out of their way, kicking up stones and skidding off the side of the road. I saw several overturned cars in ditches.

It took me almost three hours to reach Lake Charles. The civic center had been converted into a makeshift drop-in center similar in many respects to what I'd known at the Ozanam Center. Men and women sat in chairs facing a row of FEMA officials. They reminded me of people stuck in a Greyhound bus station—exhausted by delay, waiting for a schedule update. Their wet clothes clung to their bodies and puddles of dirty water widened beneath them. Buses stood outside to take evacuees out of town, but where? No one seemed to know. Behind fogged glass, I saw men, women and children looking out a bus window at those of us still inside. I think refugees, whether from a storm or a war, look the same. Lost and alone, with a mix of dread and resignation in their eyes that says their situation won't change for the better, it'll just change. They've crossed an invisible line, and their future—what they have of one—won't be known for some time.

I interviewed a man who complained that the police had rousted him out of his house without giving him time to take anything other than a pack of cigarettes. What about pictures of my dead wife? he said. My children? A woman said an oak tree fell on her roof, nearly splitting her small house in two. The hurricane, she continued, sounded like an infant screaming.

The rain continued falling in sheets, and floodwaters spread into downtown Lake Charles. I left the civic center while the roads were still passable and stopped at a gas station. Drivers mobbed the station's convenience store demanding supplies. The clerk shook his head and backed away from the door. Raised fists pummeled the glass. I gambled that I had enough gas and left without filling up.

When I reached Gramercy, I filed my story, shut down my laptop, and listened to the wind howl. I'm done here. However, I won't return to Kansas City. Not yet. In the morning I'll drive onto I-10 once more, meld into an endless convoy of evacuees, aid trucks and military jeeps. I'll drive in the rain toward Gulfport and you.

September 26, 2005
Dear Mr. Titler:
I am turning down 47th Street in Gulfport. I pull into your driveway behind a black pickup truck and park. Looking at your house, I think of the miles I've traveled since I first wrote to you, a boy infatuated with the singular experience of a German fighter pilot. His life inspired me to write to you and to World War I veterans across the globe, and I began to imagine a world beyond my Winnetka home.

Now, decades later, I find myself reconsidering the journeys I embarked on. Mr. Titler, I am forty-eight. I have lived twenty-three years longer than Richthofen. I was twenty-five, the age he died, when the Ozanam Center hired me. Since then I have been to Afghanistan and other remote places around the world and have seen the consequences of war in the faces of people whose hopeless stares bored into me until I looked away. I've written my dispatches and moved on, but their painful stories linger like bad dreams. As H. E. Hart said of Richthofen, I am now old enough to appreciate how young too many of the dead and suffering are.

I can still see myself at the breakfast nook table, oblivious of war and its consequences, writing my first letter to you, slowly and carefully, my mother beside me. I felt very bold. At the start of something new, but I didn't know what. I feel like that boy again as I get out of my car and knock on your door.

An elderly man with thinning white hair brushed back from his forehead answers. He adjusts a pair of brown glasses and tips his head back, appraising the boy. He appears puzzled. The boy assumes that he has the wrong house.

The old man looks past the boy at neighbors cleaning their yards of branches and other debris from the hurricanes. He sees the neat piles tied in bundles at the ends of their driveways. The streets clear, cars washed of grit, plywood removed from windows. Glass sparkles in the renewed order burgeoning across the neighborhood. He turns back to the boy.

"You're taller than I thought you'd be," he says, the slow indication of a smile creasing the corners of his mouth.

"Mr. . . . Titler . . .?"

"You're thinner, too, than I imagined, but other than that you turned out just the way I thought you would."

He had read the boy's letters after he left San Francisco. Bad health and carpal tunnel defeated his efforts to reply, but he had wanted to respond, as much as he wants to say something now. He still remembers when he saw his first airplane, painted orange and black, two hundred feet over his family's house in his hometown of Altoona, Pennsylvania. How he strung model planes from his bedroom ceiling and saw every flying picture that came to town. Years later he tested for his pilot's license in an open cockpit on a frigid December afternoon.

Titler will tell the boy these stories soon enough, and the boy will tell him stories as well. They will sit in the kitchen eating slices of apple pie and catch up. The years of silence between them will fall away.

For now, they contemplate each other a moment longer. Then Titler takes the boy who read his book and gave his knowledge a value he had never considered into a deep embrace; past and present merging into the now middle-aged man he holds against him, no longer a boy although he can't help but think of him as that driven youngster, so different, really, dropping into his life the way he had through the mail, to impart one final observation.

"You made something of yourself, son. You made something of yourself."

November 2, 2005
Dear Malcolm,
I wish you luck on your New Orleans article. Oh boy, how well do I know the rush of emotions at finishing a long project; publishing hell? Yes!—just one emotional peak and crash after another. Relax; you can't miss. Keep scribbling! Best wishes, Dale

Titler and I spoke by phone and corresponded through email after I returned to Kansas City. He said he was still at work on the Glenn Miller book he had first mentioned to me in 1994. He asked if I knew of any publishing houses that might be interested. Some editors I knew had the kind of connections he sought. They suggested some outlets, and I passed them along to him. After so many years of asking for his guidance, I felt honored to help.

October 14, 2006
Hello Malcolm,
I don't know where this email will find you; possibly you may still be in Afghanistan or on assignment elsewhere in the world. But I thought it was time I got back to you, as I have been much remiss in my correspondence. I have, in fact, somehow misplaced your latest email to me.
I regret to say I have not followed through with your kind pointer on the Sandra Dijkstra Literary Agency and your effort on my behalf. It was most kind of you to go to bat for me. Despite the promise it holds, I have all but lost total interest in pursuing the Glenn Miller issue. I'm eighty now, and after more than thirty years of striving with the mystery [of Miller's death], I'm ready to throw in the towel and enjoy my

declining years. Struggling with publishers and editors no longer holds my interest as it once did. I have come to grips with the realization that the writers do not produce those readable, salable and entertaining works that make it to market; the publishers do that—and they are in complete control. And publishers, being human, make a lot of mistakes.

More than a year after Katrina, the Coast is still pretty much of a mess. Recovery and rebuilding is agonizingly slow.

Again, I apologize for my tardy response. Email me and let me know where you are and what you're doing. I think of you often and wish you well; we'd welcome another visit should your assignments bring you into the area again. Warmest regards, Dale

* * *

I did not hear from him again. I stopped writing to him too. Work and freelance travel assignments I used vacation days to pursue overseas consumed all my time. New York literary agents read my stories and several asked if I was working on a book. I thought of little besides taking advantage of their interest and further establishing my career.

In 2008, I completed a book on Afghanistan, an endeavor that punctured my ego when more than thirty publishers rejected it before Beacon Press picked it up. My mother, then ninety-two years old, was ecstatic. "You see, you see!" she told me over the phone. "I knew you could do it. Listen to your mother!"

My triumph was short-lived. The *Star* laid me off in March 2009, a casualty of the Great Recession. My father died that May, and I returned home to Winnetka to care for my mother. The one bright spot: My Afghanistan book, *The Khaarijee: A Chronicle of Friendship and War in Kabul,* came out in September. I sent a copy to Titler, writing to him from the same desk on which I had drafted my first letter to him, but he didn't answer.

Despite my experience, my years as a reporter meant little in Chicago's tight job market, and I found no work. In one instance, my résumé was one among more than two hundred submitted for a position in the *Chicago Tribune*'s Schaumburg bureau, a suburb northwest of the city. Desperate, I took temp jobs much as I had decades earlier. In 2013, I found full-time work with the maintenance crew of a golf course at Park Ridge Country Club, near my mother's house. I was fifty-six and cutting golf tees for minimum wage. Overcome, depressed, I stopped applying for reporting jobs and quit writing. I went to bed with no expectations of the next day. In the morning, I woke up in an exhausted stupor. My journalism career was a thing of the past.

To make matters worse, my mother had changed dramatically in the short time I'd been home. Perhaps it was the shock of my father's death after sixty-two years of marriage. Perhaps I had been so preoccupied with my own problems that I'd failed to notice her decline. She no longer remembered Titler and many other people. She had arthritis and curvature of the spine, and she had lost sight in one eye. She was almost deaf. She was not so unaware, however, that she did not recognize her mental and physical diminishment. She hated her neediness. She railed against the caregivers I hired to help her—except for one, Cathy, who had grown up in rural Ireland and spoke with a brogue. She had a helmet of curly straw-colored hair and wore large round glasses that slid down her nose. She brought my mother sweet rolls and magazines. What is more important, she made her laugh.

"Malcolm says he's going out to pick up girls," Cathy shouted into my mother's ear when I'd leave for work. "He says we're not good enough for him."

Even Cathy, however, could not prevent my mother's mood swings. At times, she exhibited the anger and fitfulness of a two-year-old, and I was often the object of her ire. I did not have a Titler-like third-party source of wisdom to help me through elder care.

My first day at Park Ridge, I picked up sticks blown onto the fairways by a storm. A young man from Mexico, Santos, worked with me. He asked me my name, and I told him. Malkin, he said. He tried several times to pronounce "Malcolm" but never got it right. He apologized. Don't worry, I told him, but he wasn't satisfied. He was studying English at a community college twice a week and wanted to get it right. When he got tired of trying, he asked me if I knew Belmont Avenue in Chicago. Yes, I told him. Santos lived on Belmont. Since we both knew the street and he could pronounce it, he asked if he could call me Belmont.

"That would be fine," I said.

I wondered if he was mocking me. Maybe he meant nothing by it. He seemed nice enough. I didn't know, other than that I'd lost my job and now I'd lost my name.

One June afternoon, my third month at Park Ridge, I was assigned to clear weeds from a brick walk. I used a knife to pry the weeds loose and dropped them in a bucket. I alternated between bending over, kneeling, and squatting. My back ached no matter the position. A club member in a blue polo shirt with a purple alligator on the breast pocket and Bermuda shorts watched me work. He held a drink and a cigar.

"How long have you been here?" he asked finally.

"Just started," I said.

"Why? Do you see this as an opportunity?"

"No."

"Then why?"

I didn't answer. He walked away. He had no idea. He didn't know me, my previous life. But there was no reason he should. I kept pulling weeds.

Each evening, I drove home from Park Ridge, kissed my mother on the forehead, and asked about her day.

"Fine," she'd say. "Did you write today? Have you had dinner?"

"I'll make myself something in a minute." She didn't know I worked at a country club. She assumed I was still a reporter.

"You eat poorly," she admonished.

I went into the kitchen leaving my mother in the living room with a caregiver. After I ate, I read in my bedroom. I listened to the caregiver shout to penetrate my mother's deafness before I nodded off. Sometimes I'd awaken and hear my mother on her exercise bicycle, ninety-six years old, unable to sleep and refusing to give in to her infirmities.

The pedals creaked in strained rhythm. When she got tired, my mother spoke to my father. Can you see me, Chuck? she'd say. Are you watching? Help me for another five minutes, Chuck.

Her loneliness touched my own. I lay in bed wondering what I was going to do until three a.m., when my alarm roused me. Yawning and stretching, I got up, showered, made coffee, and smeared two slices of toast with peanut butter for breakfast. I checked email and Facebook hoping I'd have a message from a newspaper editor. Nothing. I read the *Tribune* and the *New York Times* online, then drove twenty minutes to Park Ridge and clocked in at five-thirty.

Every morning, I started my shift driving a golf cart across a path of pink pebbles and onto the rough to clean water sprinklers. The thick tires pressed into the dew-wet grass and left wide tracks, the whines of the strained engine violating the dawn. I stopped behind the swaying, low-fingered branches of a willow. The dying complaint of the cart's engine drifted into the milky morning light spreading across the sky, and a flat quiet unfolded around me. Warm dense breezes swept veils of mist rising from the night-cooled ground. Red-winged blackbirds rolled and dropped almost to the ground before rising again to chase a red-tailed hawk. The raven outline of a coyote trotted across a sand bunker and stared in my direction. Headlights from tractor mowers cutting fairways penetrated the dark like under-water creatures, and Santos and my other coworkers driving them shouted, "Yee-hah!" to one another like drovers. I cherished this time of the morning. I emerged from within its fading shadows feeling as if I were newly born and looking forward rather than backward. But at fifty-six, I knew I was not.

My second year at Park Ridge, while I was planting shrubs near the country club's entrance, I received an email from Titler's daughter, Cathy.

August 16, 2014
Dear Malcolm,
I came across your name on the internet. I must admit that I never kept track of Dad's contacts during his writing career, however I do recall hearing your name favorably in the past. I wanted to write and let you know that Dad's health has rapidly been declining since April. He fell and broke a rib on April 18th. Since then, it's been one setback after another. When I visited him today, I asked if he remembered you and he broke into a huge smile and said that he sure did. I told him I was going to email you and tell you he was under the weather. He told me to tell you hello. Sincerely, Cathy Titler

I told Cathy I'd drive down to visit her father but he died on August 20, before I could get time off. I scolded myself for not having visited him since Katrina, for allowing my work and ambition to get in the way of the small things that become big things when you can no longer do them. And given where I was working, I questioned the value of my accomplishments.

That evening, I looked through the folder of my correspondence with Titler. I reread the *Tribune* article about the Red Baron's granddaughter and thumbed through copies of my carefully handwritten letters and his patient replies. I recalled sitting at my desk by the window overlooking a terrace. Squirrels scampered across the roof. The shade thrown by the large branches of an oak patterned my desk. Watching those patterns shift and sway with the wind, I recalled writing my first letter to him. *Dear Mr. Titler.* I had no idea then that his reply would be the start of a correspondence that would last decades and influence the course of my life. Spurred by

Titler, I had learned the basic skills necessary for my working life. I chose not to think of him as gone. He was just not with me as I'd like him to be, but he was still there in the many letters I'd saved.

Five years after I returned home, my ninety-eight-year-old mother's diminished health took its cruelest toll when her legs became too weak for her to walk. With great effort, she would push herself up off the living room couch where she spent her days. She leaned forward, her legs shaking until the shuddering became too much and she collapsed back on the couch. She began using a walker and then a wheelchair.

"Dammit!" she'd shout in frustration.

On Thanksgiving morning 2015, my mother made yet another futile attempt to walk.

"Don't try to get up again," I said. "I'll get the wheelchair."

"Don't tell me what to do!" she snapped.

She stared straight ahead through the patio glass doors, infuriated. Her eyes burned with the anger of total defeat, an anger that knew there was no place to turn, no doctor, no anything that would support her desperate efforts to walk.

Fuck it.

She would never have said that—often reprimanded me for my liberal use of four-letter words—but that was what her look said to me. *Fuck it. If I have to live like this, I won't.*

She did not talk the rest of the day. Her expression changed from exasperation to an impenetrable calm that stayed with her into the following morning. A nurse came by and listened to her heart, checked her blood pressure. Everything fine.

The next morning, November 28, my mother woke up feeling exhausted. Cathy helped her out of bed. She'd never seen my mother so weak, she told me. My mother didn't shower. She consented to her wheelchair without complaint. She ate a full breakfast, however, alleviating my concern: two scrambled eggs, a pork sausage, sliced tomato and two pieces of wheat toast. She read the *Chicago Tribune*.

I drove to the supermarket and picked up some seedless grapes, her favorite. She said nothing when I offered them to her. Cathy suggested that she nap. She helped my mother into the wheelchair and pushed her down the front hall to her room.

My mother got into bed, lay on her side, and fell asleep within seconds. Cathy put a blanket over her and tucked it in. She took off my mother's shoes. She watched her breathing for some time, growing more and more concerned. She called for me. I heard the urgency in her voice and hurried down the hall. I listened to my mother take two shallow breaths and then one deep breath. Two shallow, one deep. Two shallow, one deep. Soon the deep breath became shorter and less pronounced. My thoughts flashed to Kabul. In 2012, I found a cat that had been hit by a car. I took it to my hotel room. It breathed the same way before it died.

"Oh, Letty," Cathy said, her voice breaking. "Oh, Letty, don't go."

I stared at my mother. Her eyes closed, mouth open a crack. Her chest no longer rising and falling. I touched her forehead and brushed away hair fallen across her face. I wiped a drop of saliva from a corner of her mouth. For no good reason, I'd always assumed we'd have a moment together before she died. That I would sit beside her, holding her hand perhaps, listening to her final words before she drifted off. Instead, she had released me without notice. In that moment, I could not remember my frustration with her, could not recall how her neediness at times annoyed me to distraction. I felt unmoored, too stunned for tears. I called to her.

"Mom!"

As if I could summon her back.

"Mom!"

After my mother died, I returned to Kansas City in the hope that my work with the *Star* would land me a journalism job, but I had been gone a long time. My connections had pretty much dried up. Again, I supported myself through temp jobs.

Then Bill Bell, a former *Philadelphia Inquirer* colleague teaching journalism at the University of Missouri–Kansas City, asked me to speak to his class. I turned him down. Who was I to talk to aspiring reporters? I thought. He asked me to reconsider.

I recalled when Titler had written, *Not to throw a damper on your efforts, but I have given up writing.* I understood how discouraged he must have felt. The sense of total defeat that leaves you slumped in a chair, unable to move, the very notion of getting up an insuperable task. Yet despite what he said, he had gotten up. He didn't stop writing until much later. Even toward the end of his life, his family told me, he had continued jotting down ideas, continued revising his Glenn Miller manuscript. He persevered.

I think you have the spark and drive to accomplish what you want in the world, Malcolm, he had written in 1980. *Don't try to get it all at once, however. Remember that living is the reason for life. The important thing is to keep going.*

I spoke to Bill's students. I told them about my mother and how she had made my brothers and me read and write, and how she had pushed us to ask questions. I brought up Titler and explained how his book had laid the foundation for me becoming a reporter and traveling abroad. Rather than focusing on the famous, I explained that my work in social services had inspired me to examine often ignored lives. The people I wrote about weren't well known like Richthofen. They didn't fit a news cycle. They lived day to day with few options to choose from other than bad and less bad, but to a person they never buckled under.

"Neither would I," I said.

The next morning, I woke up determined to write. Write something. I didn't know what. Just write. Interview someone at a bus shelter, a coffee shop, anybody. I had to rekindle the hunger and motivation that had been lost to me for too long.

I showered, dressed, and drank a cup of coffee. I grabbed a note-pad and my jacket. Then my phone buzzed. A Facebook message:

Dear Mr. Garcia, I'm a student of Bill's. We met in class. There is talk of a national strike on May Day and I am going to NYC where some good things might work out and I want to write about it. Would you be available to talk?

Yes, I wrote. *I'd be happy to.*

Draft Notice

(1968)

In 1968, at the height of the Vietnam War, my Republican parents had no patience with draft dodgers or any other critics of the war. They believed that if Saigon fell to communism, all of Southeast Asia would collapse with it. Draft dodgers should be jailed and anyone who burned the flag should be jailed with them. But when my mother read in the *Chicago Tribune* about young men from Winnetka who had been drafted, she openly suggested, with no apparent awareness of her own about-face, that my older brother, Butch, avoid the draft. She would, she said, send him to Mexico to live with her sister.

"I don't think we have to worry," my father said one Saturday morning in the breakfast nook as he drank tea with one hand and held a copy of the *Tribune* in the other. My mother had just gotten off the phone with her friend Joanie. Joanie knew of a young man in the nearby suburb of Wilmette who had just been drafted.

"I'm just saying," my mother replied, walking back to the table.

My mother's politics weren't conclusions she had reached on her own, but were conservative values handed down from one generation of her family to the next and accepted without question. Her father had hoped Charles Lindbergh would run against Franklin Roosevelt for president. He also supported the internment of Japanese Americans during World War II. My mother defended his positions more than twenty years later at our dinner table while she and my father rolled their eyes at news stories about hippies and the drug culture of Haight-Ashbury.

"Those teenagers should use their money to get an education," she said.

My mother believed that a woman should stay home with her children and thought day-care programs broke up families. She ran errands while my brothers and I were in school, but was always back by the time we came home. Without fail the phone would ring as she was rushing to unpack grocery bags, fix us a snack, and begin preparing dinner.

"Lord, I've been gone all day, and I have a thousand and one things to do before I get dinner going. I can't talk to anyone now!"

She would dash through the kitchen and out the screen door to the backyard, thrashing the air above her head with her hands, and instruct me to say that she was out. She would stand on her tiptoes and frame her face against the screen door, mouthing "Who is it?" as I explained that my mother was out, and no, she shouldn't be gone too long.

When it came to her family, however, my mother thought for herself. Butch, Michael, and I were her children, and she would protect us despite her political beliefs. As for her father, he could just roll in his grave.

"It's such a shame," my mother said, reflecting on her conversation with Joanie.

My father nodded. I reached across the table for the bowl of sugar for my cereal.

"Ask, don't reach," my mother scolded.

That afternoon I rode my bike to my friend Tom's house. Michael left at the same time to see one of his friends. When I got home a few hours later, I ran into the kitchen, eager for something to eat. My mother stood by the counter, sorting the day's mail.

"Can I have a cookie?" I asked.

"May I," my mother corrected.

"May I?"

"Wash your hands."

My mother kissed me on the forehead. I grabbed a cookie and then took my two jars of inchworms off the kitchen windowsill.

"Look," I said, pointing at the leaves they'd gnawed.

My mother didn't hear me. Holding one letter, she walked through the living room to the foot of the stairs.

"Chuck," she called to my father. "Oh, Chuck? There's a letter here from the draft board. It's for Butch."

I could hear my father's voice but couldn't make out what he was saying.

"All right," said my mother.

She walked back into the kitchen and began unloading the dishwasher. Then she went into the living room and sat down, staring at the floor. I knew something was wrong but didn't understand what. I kept quiet and my mother did too, and together we waited for my father.

When he came downstairs, my mother got up and gave him the letter. He turned the envelope over in his hands.

"You haven't opened it?"

"What are you talking about?"

"Open it."

"It's not mine to open."

"Then we don't know. We don't know what it might be."

"It's from the draft board, Chuck, for Lord's sake!" my mother snapped, jabbing a finger at the return address.

"Where's Butch?" he said.

"He's out with Andy," she said. I didn't like Andy. He had thrown stones at me when I was in the third grade, and I hadn't forgotten. I had been tagging along with him and Butch when they were playing basketball in the driveway and Andy had wanted me out of the way.

"We should just open it," my father insisted.

"No."

My mother had certain rules she adhered to, no matter the circumstances. Among them was the conviction that you don't open other people's mail. She was just over five feet but she had a kind of stubbornness that made all of us, my father included, think twice about questioning her. "Listen to me, my friend," she would say in a voice deeper than our basement when one of my brothers or I pushed her too far.

However, she could not intimidate the draft board. She had no power to put it in its place. Her fear filled the kitchen. She paced and opened and closed cabinets randomly. My father bit his lower lip and drummed his fingers on the kitchen counter.

"Stop that," my mother told him.

"I think we should just open the letter," my father repeated.

"No," my mother said.

"Well then, find Butch. Call Andy's house."

"You call his house if you want, Chuck."

"Christ almighty, do you just want to worry?"

"I said, if you want, call him."

My father looked at me. "Go outside while your mother and I are talking," he said.

"Don't leave the driveway," my mother warned.

"Mom!"

"This is not the time to argue," my father said.

I hurried outside. It was early afternoon and quiet. A patrol car drove slowly past our house. The officer waved and I held up my arm and he disappeared behind trees. I listened to the fading sound of his car until I no longer heard it. I thought of Butch. I wondered what would happen to him. I had an art teacher who was drafted. Mr. Simoneck didn't return to school after Christmas break. A substitute took over for him.

"Mr. Simoneck has been called away," the principal, Mr. Becker, told us.

My father had served in the navy in World War II. His ship was to have participated in the invasion of Japan, until the atomic bomb fell on Hiroshima. I had seen enough John Wayne war movies on television to think that my father would have wanted to go to war and kill Japs and be a hero. I had killed hundreds of them myself, playing outside with imaginary machine guns. I was disappointed when my father said he was glad he didn't go to Japan. Now it sounded as if Butch would go to Vietnam. I wondered whether he wanted to, or like my father would rather not. I didn't like the fear in my mother's voice and the way she and my father snapped at each other. I wished Andy would get drafted.

A car stopped in front of the driveway and Butch got out. Andy was behind the steering wheel. Butch walked over and rubbed my head, something he liked to do in front of his friends. It made me feel small, and I ducked away from him. He was tall and thin, with a mop of brown hair and narrow sideburns. He wanted to grow a mustache, but so far only blond fuzz showed beneath his nose.

"What's going on, Moose?" he asked.

He had begun calling me Moose when I was born. Neither he nor my mother knew why, but the name stuck, just as Butch had stuck to him.

"Nothing," I said. "You got some mail."

"Mail?"

"Yeah."

"How would you know?"

"I saw Mom go through it."

"Who from?"

"I don't know. She says it's from the draft board."

He stared at me. "I thought you didn't know."

I followed him into the house. I heard my father still tapping his fingers against the breakfast nook table. He and my mother hadn't moved. They both looked in our direction.

"What's wrong?" Butch asked.

"You have a letter," my mother said, sounding not like my mother at all but someone whose voice was coming from another part of the house.

"We don't know what it is," my father said, giving Butch the envelope.

"We won't let anything happen to you," my mother assured him.

Butch scowled, looked at the envelope and then at my mother and father. They watched him. My mother's eyes began to tear up, and she asked me to hand her her purse. She dug around in it until she found her sunglasses and put them on.

"Just open it," my father said. "We can't do anything until we know what they want."

"We know what they want," my mother said.

"Open it."

"Leave him alone."

Butch turned the envelope over in his hands. He found a corner by the flap that wasn't glued and wiggled his little finger into the gap. His hands shook. I tried peering over his shoulder and he shot me a look. The silence in the kitchen, fragile as glass. Butch worked his finger along the length of the envelope until he could tear it open. He pulled the letter out, and it dropped onto the floor. He wiped his hands on his pants, picked it up, and read it. After a moment, he let out a sigh. "It's a form letter."

"Let's see that," my father said.

Butch gave him the letter and my father put on his glasses. Butch sat down and pressed his face into his hands.

"Letty . . . it's a change of address form," my father observed. He voice was tense. He tried to hide his annoyance. "They're updating their records. In case he had moved. That's all. Look."

He held it out to her. She read it and then turned her back. Her shoulders shook. She stared out the window at the spot she used to watch when I would play in the driveway. She took off her sunglasses and reached for a Kleenex. Then she walked into the dining room and we heard the muffled sounds of her crying as she went upstairs. My father gave Butch the letter and followed her.

"Letty . . ." he said, his voice trailing off.

I don't remember what we did that night. I imagine that Butch, Michael, and I set the dinner table as usual and waited for my father to fill our plates in the kitchen. We would have taken them into the dining room and stood by our chairs until our mother sat down. I'm sure she reminded us to keep our elbows off the table and to sit straight. We would have cleared the table after dinner. Later, my father would have watched the ten o'clock news while my mother paid bills in the kitchen. The letter, I know, was not discussed then or ever again.

Butch never went to Vietnam, and the war had all but ended when Michael and I were old enough to register for the draft. Unlike so many other young men, my brothers and I were spared.

When I visit home now, Butch and I get together at his house in Glenview, Illinois, not far from where our parents live. We drink beers, discuss the news, and take political positions. He's a Republican. I'm a Democrat in the George McGovern mold. We have new wars. He recalls the draft.

"After you signed up for the draft, they threw all the birthdays into a hopper," he told me. "Depending where you lived, the pool was larger or smaller. I was lucky. My pool included all the suburbs around us. In the lottery, my birthday was 161. It was listed in the newspaper. They never called me up, though."

American GIs seemed so old when I was a kid watching the war on the news. *And that's the way it is, March 16th, 1968,* Walter Cronkite would intone. Now I'm at least twice the age of the average grunt.

These days, Butch cautions me not to accept any more reporting assignments in Afghanistan.

"And definitely don't go to Iraq," he says.

He supports both wars, as do our parents, but they would be frantic if I returned to Kabul or went to Baghdad.

When I took my sixth trip to Kabul, in 2005, I told Butch but not our parents. He asked me if I was trying to get myself killed, but I returned in one piece as I'd assured him I would. Ironically, he died a year later of congestive heart failure.

I have not experienced combat. I did see the body of an Afghan farmer killed by a mine in 2002 on the road to Bagram Air Base. He looked like he was sleeping while the lower half of his body drained into the hard soil. His donkey, untouched, brayed just feet away.

In the summer, when I see people stretched out on beach towels tanning their backs, heads rolled to one side, eyes closed, I'll sometimes think of that farmer. I'll see him. The way he was on the ground under the sun, clear blue skies all around. I'll hear his donkey too.

I go about my days propped up by the habits of my upbringing and today's technology. My phone buzzes with text messages, emails fill my inbox, Facebook informs me of a friend's request. I expect to be surprised . . . and am grateful when I'm not.

Gypsy
(1986)

I imagine it this way.

Gypsy awakens from a restless sleep, stretches, hears his bones crack. Sees how the curtains in his room at the Cadillac Hotel absorb the light of a late afternoon on Eddy Street in San Francisco's Tenderloin district, and at that moment decides to start drinking again.

He doesn't remember having a booze dream, just woke up and decided: Today is the day I'm going to get fucked up. Something clicks into place. Thank God, it's been settled. For days he had been agitated and unable to sleep. His body ached from the weight of his bitterness. He tried to read some of his old textbooks on alcohol- ism and its treatment, tried to take pleasure in his term papers and the comments scrawled in red by his professors, *Nice insight!* and *Excellent observation!* but those evening extension classes at U. C. Berkeley had been nothing but a betrayal, an illusion of accomplish- ment, and he tossed the books and his notepads across the room with a rage that kept him awake at night. He had done everything he should, and still he was denied the promotion he deserved.

Now that he has decided to drink, he feels calm and almost falls asleep again. He folds his hands behind his head and plans. He'll do his shift at the Ozanam Center as scheduled. When he gets off, he'll wait for me. I'm interviewing for shelter director at nine. Gypsy had pushed me to apply, and he'll want to wish me well. Then he'll start drinking.

When Jim Curtis, the director of the Ozanam Center, hired me in May 1983, he assigned me to nights: 10:30 p.m. to 6:30 a.m., five days a week, Saturday to Wednesday.

My first evening, the shift supervisor, Bill Vidaver, took me up a flight of stairs to a room filled with intoxicated men and women. Some of them were shaking. Others were passed out. Still others smoked and stared at the floor as if they were ashamed. A deep brown carpet made the dimly lit space even dimmer. Six round tables took up one side of the room, and four couches provided additional places to pass out when the thirty-bed dormitory behind the kitchenette filled up.

A man with thinning black hair, a handlebar mustache, plaid shirt, jeans, and boots sat behind a desk. He glanced at me and then turned away to change stations on a radio playing Muzak.

"This is Gypsy," Bill said. "Gypsy, this is the new kid."

Gypsy looked at me again.

"I'll tell you who the assholes are around here," he said.

Still in his room at the Cadillac, Gypsy rolls a joint. He is sober. Not clean and sober. Sober, period. Not like some of the other recovering Ozanam staff who smoke dope but say they're sober *and* clean. That bugs him. The lies. He never pretends he doesn't smoke pot. Gave Little Stevie a joint one morning on Seventh Street when Stevie had the shakes so bad he couldn't walk, just rattled in place like an idling car with a bad engine. Stevie had been on the street fifteen years easy. Drinking maybe longer. He and Gypsy hung out together when Gypsy was doing his thing. A sight, the two of them. Gypsy over six feet and Little Stevie peaking at five foot four on a good day. Face dirt-streaked, scraggly goatee, mop of brown hair, long tobacco-stained fingers dancing with the jitters, Stevie, shaking uncontrollably, looks to his friend Gypsy for help.

Gypsy held the joint that morning until Stevie's body ceased quaking long enough for him to clamp his trembling lips around it. He inhaled so long and deep Gypsy thought he might burst. After another hit Stevie collapsed, higher than God, in the doorway of a used clothing store. Gypsy left him there to buy a mickey of Thunderbird at Fred's Liquor store a good two blocks away. He gave it to Stevie, who held it in both hands like an infant with a bottle of formula and downed it in four hard swallows, his Adam's apple dancing up and down his throat. Then he belched and let out a long sigh, staining the air with the venom of his breath.

"Thanks, Gypo. You loan me a dollar?"

"You pay me back?"

Stevie laughed, showing toothless gums flecked with bits of weed. Gypsy gave him two dollars, one extra for inflation, he said, and walked to work. He felt good about helping Stevie but a little ashamed too, because he felt he was better than Stevie. He had beaten booze. The framed certificates he'd accumulated from the alcoholism classes he'd completed at Berkeley hung on his walls. Maybe it wasn't superiority he felt but confidence. Maybe he was just grateful not to be in the same shape as Little Stevie. He didn't know, didn't dwell on it. He pocketed the joint and kept walking.

Hands clasped behind his head, Gypsy imagines his first swallow of Jack Daniel's. It will fill him with warmth like a spring day after a long winter, gradually spreading its heat into every muscle, until all the stiffness in his neck and shoulders vanishes and his head clears of anger. The booze will burn his throat, leave his mouth dry and in need of more. He'll order a beer and another shot of Jack, run his tongue against his teeth. He has a reservoir he needs to fill.

After Bill left, Gypsy told me about a sex addict who had tried to check into detox weeks before. The addict told Bill he went through ten male prostitutes a day. "Oh," Bill said. "Oh, oh! I can't stand it!

Give me one!" Kind of jumping in his seat as the guy described each of his encounters. "Oh! Oh! Oh! Of all my addictions, why couldn't I have had *that* one?" Bill said in a high-pitched drawl, exaggerating every syllable. At least that was the way Gypsy imitated him.

Bill was a recovering dope fiend. Been clean maybe five years, Gypsy said. Never cuts his hair, ties it off with a rubber band into a long ponytail and considers it combed for the day.

Always wears a long underwear top no matter how hot the weather and an open chamois shirt. Has enough track marks on his arm to map out a road trip. Promoted to counselor a few months back.

"Oh!" Gypsy said, imitating him again, "Oh!" and laughed some more, a light breathy laugh, and I laughed with him.

That night Gypsy told me he had started drinking in the army in the 1970s. After his discharge, he roamed the country. Drank Jack Daniel's in the back of Greyhound buses to be close to the bathroom. He would pass out, wake up, and ask the driver where they were headed. His friends started calling him Gypsy because he never stayed in one place very long before he came to California. He was thirty-seven when I met him and had been in San Francisco ten years.

"That's it," he said. "The CliffsNotes version of my life."

The police often picked up fucked-up homeless people. They slipped on plastic gloves, pulled men and women infested with lice from the back of their squad cars, and delivered them to the Ozanam Center. Intake counselors like me checked them in. They could stay twenty-four hours. Ten days had to pass before they were eligible for detox again, a rule that was little more than a token effort at preventing the detox from becoming a nightly crash pad for alcoholics. It was obvious from the thickness of the files that the majority of clients returned to the center repeatedly and saw the detox as their permanent home.

The intake took seconds to complete: name, age, when did they have their last drink, any known medical conditions. Then the client climbed the flight of stairs to detox, their steps heavy and slow until they stood swaying before Gypsy and me. We assigned them a bed, gave them a towel and soap, and pointed them to the shower.

Graffiti in the bathroom:

There is no logic to good fortune or bad.
An unpredictable randomness influences the outcome of most things.

Almost everyone admitted to detox knew Gypsy from the street. "Gypsy!" they would shout in hoarse voices ruined by cigarettes and booze. Gypsy growled back in the same tone and they would all burst out laughing, reveling in a camaraderie that came from common experience and shared ruin. Gypsy would do them favors: wash their clothes, call their families, allow them to stay in detox longer than twenty-four hours. They treated him with the joyous self-consciousness a delinquent high school student might feel visiting his favorite grammar school teacher.

Not all of them liked Gypsy. I recall one guy in particular. He was lean and all sinewy muscle and had done time in San Quentin for drug dealing. He walked stiff-legged and with his back arched in a jailhouse strut. Call his name and he'd swivel around in a hot second, perfectly balanced like a ballerina, lasering you with a what-do-you-want-look. This guy—I don't remember his name—thought Gypsy had gotten too full of himself. Who did he think he was, taking college classes? He was confident Gypsy would start drinking again because, he said, Gypsy was going nowhere. Nothing in his life had changed except his ego. Was he employed in the financial district or something? Was he hanging out with suits? Did he know anyone other than the guys he put in detox? No, Gypsy was still working the street even if it was as an intake counselor. The only difference was, he wasn't drinking.

During our shift, Gypsy often recited passages he had memorized from his textbooks, but I never had the sense he fully understood what he was saying. He had all this information in his head about alcoholism yet seemed unable to interpret it and draw conclusions or make it his own. He often lost his train of thought, and at those times began to mumble insensibly. Then, when his mind reconnected with the memorized bit, he'd speak clearly again. Most of the staff ignored him when he went off on one of his textbook monologues. They patronized him with the feigned interest adults reserve for the antics of very small children.

I don't think Gypsy picked up on their condescension. Addicts are by their nature self-centered. It's all about the next drink, the next fix, the next near disaster. In Gypsy's case it was about the next class, the next certificate, the next chance to recite data from his textbooks as if it meant something.

After a detox client had showered, we offered him or her a bowl of chicken noodle soup and a sandwich: cheese, peanut butter and jelly, or tuna fish. We stretched the soup by adding so much water that it lost its color and globs of pale fat rose to the surface like decomposing jellyfish. The sandwiches were made in the morning. By the time I came in to work they were either soggy or hard as bricks.

Twenty-four hours later, we referred clients to the Salvation Army detox—Sally's, we called it—on Harrison Street, where they remained for three additional days of drying out. From there, if they were lucky, an inpatient alcoholism program took them in. But most city programs were full, and the waiting lists could be months long. With no options other than white-knuckled sobriety, they returned to the street and we saw them again in ten days.

I gradually noticed that most of the clients who stopped drinking had a college education and a solid job history before alcohol overpowered them. Sober, they recognized they still had opportunities they could pursue. They had professional backgrounds and family support that would help them make up for the years wasted boozing.

In addition, I saw that the Ozanam Center hired most of its staff from halfway houses. They knew how to cadge drinks and drugs, and their only friends were other street hustlers. They started out like me, as intake counselors, until they were promoted to counselor, a position they kept for as long as they stayed at the center. Further advancement to an administrative position required a university degree, which most of them didn't have.

"Have you been to college?" Gypsy asked me one night.

"Yes," I told him.

He wondered if the credits from his extension courses would add up to a degree. I didn't know, and suggested he look into it. He said he would. As the senior program assistant, he expected to be promoted to counselor when a position opened.

"I'm going to run this joint one day," he said.

I imagine Gypsy staring at the ceiling of his room, waiting. He decides to resign before he starts drinking again. He won't be like some of the other staff who have fallen off and then never show up to work again. He's more responsible than that. He'll complete his shift and resign effective immediately, before he punches out and waits for me. Not much of a heads-up but it will do. They'll find someone to replace him. Everyone wants extra hours. Some guy at a halfway house will need a job. Gypsy will come back to get his final check, he doesn't know when. If he must, he'll ask someone to pick it up for him.

He looks at his watch. He has more than twelve hours to wait before he holds a Jack-filled shot glass in his hand. Twelve hours. A ways to go. He'll make up for lost time soon enough.

My first night on the job, Gypsy would not allow me a break. He wanted me to see the shift in its entirety, he said, every little thing.

I struggled to stay awake, checked on sleeping clients, and mopped the floors several times while Gypsy took a nap for two hours. Later he admitted he had been fucking with me because I was new.

He dared me one night to walk down Sixth Street on my way to work to see for myself San Francisco's skid row. I knew he was messing with me again but took him up on it to show I wasn't afraid. In the 1950s, the row was centered downtown, just south of Market Street on Howard between Third and Fourth and more or less leaching into streets and alleys for a few blocks all around. It was where most of San Francisco's chronic street alcoholics hung out during the day, bought their booze, panhandled, and slept in flophouses or doorways. The area was gentrified beginning in the 1970s with then controversial urban-renewal programs that tore down cheap housing. The result: Sixth Street between Market and Howard became the new row.

Neon lights glowed in multiple colors above triple-X arcades the night I took Gypsy's dare. Liquor stores lined both sides of the street with posters in their windows advertising ninety-nine-cent pint bottles of Night Train and Thunderbird. Dilapidated welfare hotels, once called flophouses, rose above the liquor stores, and chunks of broken plaster and shattered glass and pigeon shit speckled the sidewalks. Men lounged in doorways and poorly lit lobbies where televisions flickered in spastic bursts. I passed vacant stores, peered down gloomy alleys that echoed with the gruff voices of invisible people. I glanced into bars and saw men and women huddled together like gnomes: not speaking, staring absently, heavy-lidded and confused. They leaned forward on crutches and watched me, knowing by my determined gait that I had a destination and therefore did not belong there. People on the sidewalk clutched at me demanding change, spouting slurred words, their clothes piss-stained. I hurried the rest of the way to work.

Gypsy told me he had had his last drink at a Sixth Street bar in 1981, about two years before I moved to San Francisco. By then he had been homeless and out of work as a truck driver for about five years. Someone had snatched his shoes when he had passed out on the street earlier in the day, and he entered the bar barefoot. He sat on a stool, stared at his lap, and used his last few dollars to buy a drink. His mouth tasted like he had cleaned gutters with his tongue. Threads of saliva hung off his bottom lip and fell on his toes. A sad song was playing on a radio behind the bar.

"Fuck this," he said.

He stood up and walked out without finishing his drink. He stumbled and weaved the few blocks to the Ozanam Center and checked into detox. After twenty-four hours he was transferred to the Salvation Army. He told a counselor he wanted a program. Just Gypsy's luck, the Army's Rehabilitation Center had an opening.

On the nights when the detox was quiet and Gypsy and I sat together listening to people snore, he would sometimes whisper to himself the opening line of the Allen Ginsberg poem "Howl":

I saw the best minds of my generation destroyed by madness.

One morning after work, we went out for coffee and then walked to North Beach and City Lights Bookstore, founded by beat poet Lawrence Ferlinghetti. There Gypsy showed me books by Ginsberg and other writers who'd come to prominence in the fifties for their jazzy word riffs. Gypsy had attended some of their readings back in the 1960s. He leafed through books and read aloud to himself.

After an hour I wanted to go home and crash. Gypsy, however, was not tired. He offered to walk with me to the bus stop although I was headed in the opposite direction from where he lived. He stayed with me until I caught my bus. I sat by a window and watched him pace as if uncertain which direction to take. Eventually, I knew, he would go home and get stoned. He would then roam the streets, impelled by a restlessness that put him on autopilot, an itch he couldn't control.

On the afternoon he finished his program at the Army Rehabilitation Center, Gypsy checked into a halfway house and then spent the afternoon with his buddy Rocky at the corner of Market and Van Ness. Rocky held out a hat to passersby. Gypsy had drunk with Rocky as much as he had with Little Stevie. Rocky was a gentle man. He wore blue jeans and a T-shirt stained from constant wear and too little laundry detergent. He always wore a loopy grin that let everyone see that he was in on the joke that was his life.

Another homeless man, Alabama, sat across the street on a planter drinking a mickey of Thunderbird. He suffered fierce alcoholic seizures that spun him in violent circles before he collapsed to the ground flopping and twisting like someone electrocuted. He always had blood-stained gauze wrapped around his battered head and face from the many falls resulting from his seizures. On that day, he was to relieve Rocky every other hour to allow Rocky a turn at the wine bottle.

"Better leave me some," Rocky said, watching Alabama tip the bottle back.

Gypsy smelled Rocky's breath, the blended funk of cigarettes and wine rolled into a churning ball of foul heat, and his stomach turned. He felt the crisp newness of his shirt and jeans, the cleanliness of his body that for more than a month had experienced a shower every morning. He heard the noise of cars, the scuffing of shoes on the sidewalk, the flutter of pigeons. Gypsy tingled with the hyperaware sensation of being free of the Salvation Army. He was outside, sober, alert.

"You want a hit from 'Bama's bottle, Gypo?"

"No," Gypsy said.

He had no place to go except back to the halfway house. Sit in his room and stare at the walls, alone and sober. Attend an AA meeting. Think about how good he felt not being fucked up.

Gypsy treated our shifts as seminars on alcoholism. He was the lecturer, I the student. He told me it took three days to get alcohol completely out of the body, that alcoholism had nothing to do with the kind of alcohol one drank or how long one had been drinking or even how much alcohol one consumed. He said alcohol abuse differs from alcoholism in that it did not include extreme craving for alcohol, loss of control, or physical dependence.

He would close his eyes and crinkle his forehead, conjuring more knowledge, and then, as if unburdening himself, continue imparting all that he had memorized in the early morning hours while I struggled to stay awake.

I wonder if a question occurred to Gypsy as he sat in his room at the Cadillac: What's a shot of Jack cost? I see him stand up and run his hand through his hair, thinking. Doesn't matter. Even if a shot is dirt cheap, his money won't last. Never did before. He'll be drinking dollar bottles of Night Train and Thunderbird before the week's out. Pissing and shitting himself, too. He sees his future but remains undeterred. He has no false expectations.

He takes another hit from his joint. He glances about his room: the disheveled bed, dirty clothes on the floor, spilled ashtrays, the broken chair by the closet, crumpled cigarette packs everywhere. He has lived in the Cadillac for four years. He never changed his clothes when he was drinking unless he went to a homeless shelter and was given something new to wear. Tossed his old shit down and put on the new shit. He still does that. No one picks up the old shit now. It stays on the floor until he decides to wash it or give it to the Ozanam Center's clothes closet. Maybe today he'll do laundry. Then again, what's the point? When he gets off work he won't be going back.

I stayed on nights for two months before Curtis moved me to days at my request. I had decided to apply to San Francisco State University and earn a master's degree in social work. I would need my nights free for classes and homework.

My new shift started at 6:30 in the morning, just as Gypsy was getting off. He'd meet me downstairs and we'd sit with clients who had come in the drop-in for coffee and rolls. More often than not, Gypsy stuck around for hours talking to Little Stevie, Rocky, and Eddie Conover, one of the few clients who went by his real name. Gypsy played pinochle with them in the area where people waited for detox. He taught me how to play.

Eddie always passed out in the middle of a game and pissed himself, the piss striking the floor in a steady stream like runoff from a gutter. He was beyond waking up, and Gypsy would help me carry him to a mat to sleep it off.

When he woke up, Gypsy would ask, "You in, Eddie?"

Sometimes, on my days off, I'd meet Gypsy at the Cadillac and we'd get stoned. He showed me his term papers, all of them graded A-plus. Some were typed, others written in neat, tight script. His punctuation, grammar, and footnotes were spot-on. He pointed out his certificates. He ran a finger under the University of California logo at the top of each one to emphasize that he was not attending just any school.

"I have more certificates than anyone else at Oz," he said.

We walked the streets looped out of our minds, stopping to talk to the handful of homeless men and women who knew him. They called out to Gypsy in raspy voices I will always associate with people on the street who smoke too much and are exposed to every kind of inclement weather. Other of his acquaintances nodded silently and walked past, and Gypsy let them go without a word. He shook the ones who were passed out to see if they were asleep or dead. He doled out cigarettes and change and advised anyone who would listen to check into detox.

"I'm not eligible," Little Stevie told him one afternoon. "My ten days ain't up."

"Then just pray," Gypsy said.

"What's going to become of us, Gypo?" Little Stevie said, tears in his eyes.

"Us?" Gypsy said.

The director of the night shelter resigned about six months after I moved to days. The executive director of the St. Vincent de Paul Society posted a job announcement. Applicants needed at least two years of experience in social services, a background in alcoholism treatment, and a college degree. Intake workers and counselors complained about the education requirement because none of them could meet it. A few decided to apply anyway.

That morning, after Gypsy got off his shift, we had coffee. He was quiet at first, and I could tell he was mulling something over.

"How was your shift?" I asked.

"Quiet as hell," he said.

First of the month, everybody had their welfare and disability checks. It'd be a few days before they spent all their money and needed a place to stay.

"Yeah," I said.

Then Gypsy suggested I apply for the shelter director job. No transition, nothing, just boom, you should apply. I laughed, told him he was nuts. I didn't have the experience.

"Experience is something you pick up every day," he said. "Education takes time. I'm still not done with my classes. I don't know how long it will take. You have a college degree. You have that much."

I looked at him.

"Do it," he said.

I heard no resentment in his voice, no veiled anger toward a new colleague who also happened to be a college graduate and more than ten years his junior. I was not an alcoholic. I had never been on the street.

"Do it."

I heard in his voice the weariness of someone who had been up all night with too little to do and who was still awake and knew he would be unable to sleep for hours. Perhaps in his exhaustion he had an image of his own future and, in a moment of clarity, seeing where his life would lead, decided to pass his ambitions on to me.

The end came when a counselor position opened. Curtis thought the center needed to promote more women. Only four were on staff. He gave the job to Mary, an intake counselor who was a new employee.

I don't know how Gypsy heard about Mary. He came in that afternoon with a bicycle pack filled with his framed certificates. I wasn't there, but I heard he walked into Curtis's office and placed each certificate on his desk. He began shouting. Everyone watched him through the glass window of Curtis's office that overlooked the drop-in. Curtis waited for Gypsy to finish. Then he spoke. When he finished, he and Gypsy stared at each other for a long time before Gypsy slumped slightly. He gathered his certificates into his bicycle pack and then hesitated. He stared at the pack for a long time. Then he tossed it to the floor and walked out.

Shortly after I was hired at the Ozanam Center, I'd spoken to Curtis about the extension classes offered at Berkeley. Alcoholism was considered a disability, and Gypsy and other recovering staff were eligible for state aid. The California Department of Vocational Rehabilitation covered their tuition. I, on the other hand, would have to pay out of pocket. The classes cost $300 apiece.

"Are they worth it?" I asked Curtis.

He considered my question, looked down at his desk and then back at me. A recovering alcoholic himself, he had lost an eye some- how and had had it replaced with an artificial one that was larger than his real eye. The new eye appeared magnified, and I never knew how to look at him without staring at it. So I focused on the knot in his tie.

"I wouldn't do it," he said, finally. "You'd learn something, but for the cost all you'll get is a certificate. So what? You already have a college degree. Spend your money on grad school."

Gypsy finishes his joint, puts on his shoes. He writes a check for his rent and includes a note giving thirty days' notice. He knows the manager of the Cadillac will keep his damage deposit. Someone will clean his room, clear out his clothes, and toss everything else. He feels an odd lightness followed by a brief flash of apprehension.

He leaves the Cadillac and walks toward Leavenworth Avenue. He will cut through Civic Center Park, cross Market Street, and turn down Seventh. He knows everyone who hangs out in the park, just as he knows about every street person in San Francisco. They'll give him shit because this time he won't be generous with his change and smokes. He understands what's coming. He knows he'll go through his cigarettes and money soon enough. They won't know until later. Then they'll understand.

The Ozanam Center's board of directors interviewed me for shelter director along with seven other candidates from outside the agency. I didn't get the job. I was disappointed but also relieved. I knew I wasn't ready. In 1986 the position opened up again, and this time the board hired me.

About a week after my interview, I saw Gypsy waiting to sign into detox. He sat in a corner chair wearing a sweatshirt and jeans and a navy-blue stocking cap. His face was lined with dirt and his clothes smelled of wood smoke, as if he'd been camping. He refused to look at me. Tears streaked his grimed face. I didn't know what to say, and so I said nothing.

I look back at that moment now and think that Gypsy had no sense of himself. His emptiness was complete. Just as it was that morning he walked me to the bus stop; uncertain, walking one way and then the other, no options. He was the number of extension classes he had completed, the amount of text he had memorized. When that failed to earn him a promotion, he had nothing, and, worse, nothing mattered.

Gypsy was admitted to detox but walked out the next day. I never saw him again. Perhaps he got on a Greyhound bus and left to start over elsewhere. I hope so. I don't want to remember him as I do Little Stevie, Rocky, Alabama, Eddie Conover, and the dozens of others I admitted to detox who drank themselves to early deaths.

I prefer to remember the last time I saw him sober. I had arrived for my job interview at 8 a.m. wearing a suit and tie. A few of the staff whistled, and I couldn't help but laugh despite my nervous state. Bill gave me shit about my college degree, but wished me luck.

An Ozanam Center board member stepped out of a room on the mezzanine and called my name. I stood, rubbed my sweating palms against my pants. Halfway up the stairs I glanced down and saw Gypsy emerge from the drop-in. I wouldn't know until the next day that he had completed his final shift and delivered his resignation letter. He was wearing a leather jacket, plaid shirt, jeans, and polished brown boots. Hair slicked to one side, his gunfighter mustache trimmed to perfection. He raised a hand and I waved back.

The board member gestured to me and Gypsy nodded encouragement. I continued up the stairs. I looked back one last time to see Gypsy push open a side door and turn right, toward Sixth Street.

Stabbing Johnny
(1987)

About a year after Bill stabbed Johnny in the neck, Randy began drinking again. I won't blame Randy's drinking on Bill, but he did change Randy's life and mine. If Bill hadn't stabbed Johnny, I wouldn't have left the Ozanam Center and Randy would not have been promoted to shelter director. The rest of it, Randy's ex getting sick—well, no one saw that coming any more than we anticipated Bill stabbing Johnny.

All of this happened more than thirty years ago, but here I am, still living a life undestroyed by the things that claimed so many others, thankful I was spared their problems but burdened all the same with loss and regret.

I met Randy in 1985. He was an intake counselor. That year I had been promoted to social worker, helping homeless people apply for benefits. I answered to the shelter director.

Randy had recently graduated from an alcoholism treatment program in Redwood City, about a forty-five-minute drive south of San Francisco. Although he was fifty-six, his years of drinking had not aged him. Lines did not crease his face, no gray in his blond hair. He smoked two packs of cigarettes a day. He had been married and divorced three times and was seeing his first wife, Susan, an insurance agent in Gilroy, again. They got together at her house on his days off. Sometimes the three of us would catch a movie together.

On a Wednesday around five in the morning in November 1986, Bill and Johnny requested detox. Their fat dog-eared files testified to the dozens of times they had been through detox. Bill stood about six feet tall. He always wore blue jeans, a light brown leather jacket, and cowboy boots. His thinning black hair tumbled over his forehead and a handlebar mustache framed his mouth. He walked with quick stiff strides, and he had an unpredictable temper. He never looked at you when he spoke, but past you, his glance curving around the side of your face. Johnny was the Mutt to Bill's Jeff: short and pudgy, a harmless follower. He wore two wool shirts and a couple of pairs of pants at a time no matter the weather, and a pair of sneakers. He smelled of his own funk and the damp grass where he slept.

An intake counselor asked Bill and Johnny if they had anything they wanted locked up. Bill gave him some change and a radio held together with duct tape. The counselor wrote Bill's name on a piece of paper, stuck it to the radio, put it inside a closet, and locked the doors. He then assigned them beds. A few people in the dormitory knew Bill and Johnny and greeted them in voices that sounded like the strained barking of old dogs.

Three hours later Bill asked to check out. It was close to six in the morning, so the liquor stores on Sixth Street would open soon. Bill asked for his radio and change. The counselor gave them to him and Bill left, Johnny following him. They walked four blocks to Sixth Street, San Francisco's skid row, and pooled their money. The damp air laced with car exhaust and the odor of garbage held an acrid stink that clung to Fred's Liquor Store as they entered it.

As Johnny told me later, they bought two fifths of Thunderbird wine, wandered over to the Bryant Street overpass, and drank. Johnny closed his eyes. He thought of those National Geographic specials he had watched in the Salvation Army shelter a couple of weeks before, of rushing rivers funneling into canyons, curving around rocks, all foaming and splashing, and he opened his eyes and realized he had pissed himself. He told Bill, and Bill laughed. Johnny's mood shifted and just like that he was furious. He stood up, grabbed Bill's radio, and made like he was about to throw it in his face. Bill scrambled to his feet and balled his big hands into fists. He moved on Johnny fast. Johnny froze. Then, still clutching the radio and with Bill almost on top of him, Johnny screamed and bolted back toward the center.

Two hours after Bill and Johnny left detox, I was standing at the front door of the center signing people in on a clipboard. I noticed Randy clocking in to work. Then Johnny barged shrieking through the front door with a radio clasped to his chest. I stepped back just as Bill ran in behind him and threw him to the floor. He jerked Johnny onto his back and held him by the throat. Johnny made squealing noises and rolled his head, and Bill swung his right arm back and I saw the pointed tip of a knife blade sticking out from his hand.

"Give me my radio!" Bill shouted, and plunged the blade into the right side of Johnny's neck.

"I need backup!" I yelled.

A homeless guy with a shaved head ran toward me from the drop-in area and tackled Bill. I heard the blare of approaching sirens and knew one of the intake workers had called the police. Two squad cars pulled up outside. A cop stepped out of the lead cruiser and another cop followed him inside. The first cop looked at Bill and the guy holding him, then turned toward Johnny and saw the blood from his neck pooling on the floor. The second cop applied gauze to the wound while the first cop called for an ambulance. Then he turned back to Bill and saw the knife on the floor, the thin blade sticking out from a handle wrapped in rubber bands.

"What happened?" he said.

"He stole my radio and I stabbed him, that's it," Bill said so matter-of-factly that he sounded almost reasonable.

The cop asked me and the guy holding Bill what we'd seen. As we answered, an ambulance parked behind the squad cars and two medics walked in. The cop motioned with his chin toward Johnny. The medics wrapped his neck with gauze, put him on a gurney, and wheeled him outside.

"Okay," the cop said to us.

He put away his notebook, picked up Bill's knife, and dropped it in a plastic bag. He handcuffed Bill and took him outside, his partner following him. They didn't bother with the radio. The guy who had tackled Bill asked me if he could have it.

"Sure," I said.

After the police and ambulance left, Randy and I walked to Civic Center Plaza and bought coffee. I told him it bothered me that I hadn't tackled Bill like that other guy did, that all I had done was yell for help.

Randy laughed. I must have seemed very young to him, a twenty-six-year-old who still judged himself by the rules of the playground. Randy was a middle-aged man who could consider with clear eyes the many years of his life wasted by booze and how far he had come a year into his recovery. He had a job, an ex-wife willing to give him a second chance, and enough money after rent for clothes, food, and a bus ticket to Santa Clara. He felt good.

Johnny stayed in the hospital two days. Bill had just missed an artery. When he was discharged, Johnny asked for a taxi voucher and caught a cab to the Ozanam Center. He spent his days playing pinochle with guys waiting to get into detox. At night he helped set up the shelter with the dozens of exercise mats that served as beds. Drawings of buxom women decorated the mats, and sometimes when Johnny would trace one of the figures with a finger,

I wondered if he was thinking of an ex-girlfriend or an ex-wife or anyone at all.

He left the center only to eat. He wasn't drinking.

Two weeks after his discharge from the hospital, Johnny and I were subpoenaed to testify at Bill's trial, the summons served to us in the drop-in center. Johnny testified first while I waited in the hall outside the courtroom and looked through the crack in the door. He sat on the right side of the judge, hunched forward, pale and skittish. I couldn't hear him but I saw the back of Bill's head and the orange collar of his prison jumpsuit.

Then I took the stand. I described to a district attorney how Bill had wrestled Johnny to the floor and stabbed him. The public defender representing Bill did not question me. When the judge dismissed me, I stepped down and walked around the desk where Bill sat. He drew a finger across his throat and scratched at a mole as if he meant nothing by it.

He was sentenced to nine months in San Bruno County Jail.

I didn't spend much time worrying about Bill. I had other things on my mind. The center's shelter director, John Staley, had open-heart surgery and took a two-month leave of absence. The executive director of St. Vincent de Paul, Ken Reggio, asked me to fill in. I had applied for the shelter director job in 1984, but the board of directors had chosen John.

Now, with little notice, I was responsible for a dozen shelter staff who often didn't show up for work or were drunk when they did. Staley had tolerated their behavior. A recovering alcoholic himself, he understood what I did not—that no matter what a bunch of screw-ups his staff might be, they weren't on the street because they had jobs. That counted for something. Not everyone, Staley knew, attains the purest sobriety.

I, however, saw an opportunity to make an impression. When a staff member came in late or didn't show up or stank of alcohol, I fired him. No warning, just you're out. By the end of my first week on the job, the shelter had an entirely new staff. Reggio took notice. He fired Staley and recommended me to the board of directors, who hired me.

I offered Randy my old social worker job. He was responsible, thorough, and well liked. He was also my friend. He accepted. His first clients included the shelter staff I had fired. He helped them apply for unemployment.

From my new office above the drop-in I'd see Johnny playing pinochle at a table near a stack of exercise mats in a corner. Guys hit him up for change and cigarettes, but he didn't go with them to the liquor stores. He rarely left the center. He felt better than he had in a long time, he told me, but he no longer felt like himself. Something was absent. He didn't know what it was, but he knew if he had a drink, he'd find it.

Bill completed his sentence in July 1988. When he was released he caught a bus to San Francisco and walked to Sixth Street. That night he came to the center and requested detox.

The next morning, Reggio asked me to walk a new St. Vincent de Paul board member through the center. I introduced him to the intake counselors and some volunteers, including Johnny, who were serving coffee. When I took the board member upstairs to the detox, I saw Bill sitting at one of the tables. He had put on weight. The waxy whiteness of his skin shone beneath the ceiling light. He noticed me and stood up. I didn't move. He pointed a finger at my temple. My heart rose to my throat.

"Bang," he said.

After I walked the board member to his car, I hurried over to the coffee bar and pulled Johnny aside.

"Bill's out," I told him.

"You seen him?"

"He's in detox."

I think at that moment Johnny experienced fear and relief. He had been living in the center twenty-four/seven, avoiding the temptations of the world outside for months. He must have known that one day his refuge would be breached. Maybe that had been his plan all along. Waiting for the breach. The trigger, AA members call it. A reason to drink again.

Then again, he may have thought nothing like that. What I do know is that he walked out from behind the coffee bar and I never saw him again.

I started thinking about a change myself. Weeks earlier, Robert Tobin, the executive director of Hospitality House, a homeless services agency in the Tenderloin, had asked me to apply to be director of the Tenderloin Self-Help Center, a program he had developed to help the homeless mentally ill. I had declined the offer because I had only recently become shelter director.

The people who came to the Ozanam Center rarely ventured north of Market into the Tenderloin, a gritty downtown neighborhood wedged between tourist-friendly Union Square and City Hall. Dope fiends called the Tenderloin home. Alcoholics stayed south of Market, close to Sixth Street. I knew I wouldn't see Bill in the Tenderloin.

When I called Tobin and told him I'd take the job, he didn't ask why I'd changed my mind. I gave my notice and encouraged Randy to apply for shelter director. He considered the responsibility and the stress that would come with it and where that stress might lead. Still, he applied and was hired.

"I'm ready for this," he told me.

Six months after Randy became shelter director, his ex-wife came down with what she thought was stomach flu. Susan couldn't keep food down and experienced painful spasms. Her doctor performed an upper endoscopy and made a diagnosis: stomach cancer.

He told me later how that weekend he and Susan sat on the

couch in the living room of her house. Randy absorbing the news. Evening. The curtains closed, Susan crying. Two lamps on the end table, dim yellow light. The TV turned off. The distant drone of an airplane, cars passing by on the street. The odd creaks and groans of the house and the low hum of cicadas.

Randy had drunk himself out of job after job. As shelter director he earned just $22,000 a year. When he turned sixty-five, he knew he would receive next to nothing from Social Security.

He took Susan's hand. She looked at him. He inhaled and said that without her he would need something to fall back on. It wasn't about the money. It was about managing his life without her. He paused a long time before he asked her to name him her beneficiary.

I can't imagine her reaction, dying a slow, painful death, as aware as Randy of the wasted years, only more so now that she would have no future with him to put those years deep into the past. And here Randy sat asking her to take care of him beyond the grave. No, I can't imagine. But I do understand why she told him in a rising voice to leave her house. Now. Go now, Randy. That's all you have to say? How dare you! Get out!

He left for San Francisco that night.

The next morning Randy called me, sounding out of breath and panicked. He asked me to meet him at Geary Boulevard and Leavenworth Street. When I got there, I saw him slouched against a bus shelter near a liquor store and a strip joint. Mud smeared on one side of his face and his disheveled clothes. His breath reeked of booze. I stared at him. I had no words.

"Susan makes me so mad," he said.

Without another word he left, lurching on and off the sidewalk as he made his way south toward Market Street.

Susan died soon after Randy began drinking again. I looked for him, even wandered Sixth Street all the while praying I didn't run into Bill. I called people he knew. Nothing. Eventually I gave up and tried putting him out of my mind. I felt so naive. Randy had been a recovering alcoholic and embodied all the risks those two words conveyed every day. Among my clients, I had seen many alcoholics graduate from treatment programs only to start drinking again, but I had been unable to imagine Randy giving in to his own impulses in the same way. I thought of him as a recovered alcoholic, not a recovering one. I'd not anticipated losing him. I felt betrayed.

I never expected to see Randy again and I didn't, but two years later he called me at work. He said he had stopped drinking and had a job in a San Jose homeless shelter, I don't recall the name. He was also engaged to a woman from Healdsburg, a good three-hour drive north of San Jose. He stayed with her on his days off. He suggested the three of us have dinner.

He spoke as if no time had elapsed and nothing out of the ordinary had happened since we last saw each other, and that made me furious. *Did it occur to you that maybe, just maybe, your friends have been worried about you?* I wanted to say. Instead, I made excuses. *No, I can't see you this weekend. No, next weekend is out too.* I didn't trust his sobriety. I didn't trust him. After a while, he no longer called. Months passed. Then his fiancée left a message. Randy's two-pack-a-day smoking habit had caught up with him and he had died of throat cancer. Like other alcoholics I'd met and grown close to at the Ozanam Center, life, recovery, and death had happened again.

I no longer work with homeless people. In 1997, I quit social services for journalism. I like the detachment of reporting, of participating in someone's life one step removed. I sit across from the people I interview, my notepad a bulwark between us. I ask questions, jot down answers, and write a story. I rarely see them again.

I hope Johnny stayed sober. I hope Bill stopped drinking. I hope I have the courage now to confront friends when they falter rather than avoid them. I hope, but have little certainty that any of us change that much. I consider Bill, Johnny, and Randy with an awareness I could not possibly have had when I was at the Ozanam Center, a few years out of college and working with people almost twice my age whose problems I did not share and who had hit the lowest rung of their personal hell. Recovery, digging out and up and back, was a distant galaxy to most of them. Down, really down, was their life, just as begging on the street was for the war widows and their children I met years later in Kabul. Securing the next pint or finding enough rice to eat, that was life.

Unexpected moments remind me of my time at the Ozanam Center. The other night about seven o'clock, I saw a homeless man outside a gas station on Grand Boulevard, across the street from the *Kansas City Star*. He wore mismatched work boots, shorts, and a corduroy coat stained with bird shit. No shirt. A bottle stuck out of a torn pocket. He shifted from foot to foot and kept rubbing his hands together against the damp. He asked passersby for change. He was someone Randy and I would have admitted into detox back when I was younger and thought the problems that would trip us up later only affected the people we wanted to help.

Now I watched him walk away.

Granny
(1988–1994)

Her name was Marcella Brooks, but everyone called her Granny. I would see her sitting in her wheelchair in the doorway of a boarded-up Walgreens on Market Street near San Francisco's Civic Center Plaza, a ragged brown-and-white dog named Missy sprawled across a yellow blanket in her lap. Granny's eyes would be closed, mouth open a crack. She wore tennis shoes and at least three socks on each foot. Long underwear showed beneath the hem of her dress and a wool cap covered her gray hair. The handwritten cardboard sign around her neck—"Help the Homeless"—made passersby pause. A downward tilt at the corners of her mouth even in sleep suggested that Granny disapproved of those who stopped and stared. Some of them dropped change in a cup by her feet, unaware that she received a thousand dollars a month in Social Security benefits, money she spent renting four storage lockers. Engulfed in a heavy winter coat, Granny looked smaller than she was and gave the impression that at any moment the damp, hard winds rising off the San Francisco Bay might whisk her away.

At the time I knew Granny, in the early 1990s, I was the director of the Tenderloin Self-Help Center. We were supposed to serve San Francisco's homeless mentally ill, but really we assisted anyone who walked through our doors. Most of our clients—"participants," we called them—were alcoholics, drug addicts, prostitutes, and homeless Vietnam and Gulf War combat veterans. All of them could probably have said they had a mental illness: schizophrenia, post-traumatic stress disorder, depression, bipolar disorder, or one yet unnamed that defied categorization. They had been triaged out of most social-service agencies because they required too much help, effort that most likely would not have resulted in an outcome positive enough to share with potential donors. They were difficult, cantankerous, and at times violent. They had burned through most available rehabilitation programs. They weren't going to find jobs, and if they did, they weren't going to keep them and would spend what money they earned on booze and drugs before they ever paid the rent. They had big hearts and wanted to be liked and to be useful, but they believed failure to be the inevitable outcome of any endeavor, so why even try?

Despite all this, I hired many of our participants to work at the center and signed up many more as volunteers. My reasons were simple: they knew the bureaucracy of the city's social-services system better than me, and therefore were the best ones to guide other homeless people through it. I like to think that from this task they derived a sense of satisfaction and accomplishment. The self-help center was a place people entered, found solace for a while, and then left.

Granny came to the center every morning for coffee. She used her wheelchair like a walker, standing behind it and pushing it through Civic Center Plaza and uphill toward our building with the dog in the seat, stuffed plastic bags bouncing against the chair's worn wheels. Seeing me, she would stop, shake her head, and let out a long breath as if to say, *Isn't this something?*

One day climbing the hill proved too much for Granny. At first none of us realized anything was wrong. She pushed her wheelchair into the center and parked it by the front desk, as she always did. The front-desk supervisor, "Poppa" Ron, asked her to sign in, but she said, "Shoo. Everyone knows me."

Ron had grown up in the Ozarks and always wore a floppy leather hat and cowboy boots. He'd fought in the Korean War and had come to San Francisco after being discharged from the army. He called his glasses "spectacles," said "y'all" and "I declare," and thought billboards spouting Scripture were as natural as trees. Ron got the name Poppa from the homeless teens he helped. He gave them a dollar here and a dollar there and sometimes let them crash in his battered 1970s station wagon, sagging on bald tires in front of the Lyric Hotel, where he lived. But he never let the kids into his room, where he drank and passed out. Ron wasn't a predator, just an old man who wanted to be needed.

"Get you some coffee, Granny," Ron said.

Granny wagged an arthritic finger knotted with three silver rings at her dog, telling it to stay. Free of her wheelchair, she moved in a kind of forward-leaning, jittery shuffle that picked up speed with each hesitant step and gave the impression of an impending fall. She passed through the drop-in center, a combination waiting room and hang-out area for people who were between appointments or had no other place to go. Men and women were eating day-old doughnuts there and shouting to one another as if they were miles apart. Finally, Granny made it to the small kitchen where Doug, a volunteer, asked how she wanted her coffee.

"Black," Granny said, breathless, as if she had run a block.

Doug reached for a foam cup on a shelf above the coffee machine. He got a monthly disability check and rented a studio apartment in the Tenderloin with his brother, Paul, also a volunteer. Like Granny, Paul shuffled rather than walked. He was perpetually stooped and staring at the floor, and saliva hung from his protruding lower lip. Paul suffered from stomach ailments that gave birth to farts so prodigious they would raise him to his feet if he was sitting down. He seemed oblivious of the effect this had on anyone near him and didn't understand why the others had dubbed him "Napalm." One time, Granny walked into the restroom after Paul had used it. The door had no more closed behind her when it burst open again, and Granny trundled right back out holding her nose and gasping, which explained why people left the center to relieve themselves rather than be exposed to what Paul had wrought.

Now Paul was standing behind Doug and mopping the floor as Doug poured Granny some coffee, careful not to spill any on his clothes. He liked to dress formally in black pants and white button-down shirts with starched collars. He dyed his gray hair a bright orange-red and combed it back from his forehead, parting it in the middle. He even wore a metal name tag he had paid for himself. To anyone who asked, Doug explained that he was not just a volunteer but the kitchen supervisor. But because he had a speech impediment, he pronounced "supervisor" *stupivisor*, and no one gave him the respect he felt he deserved.

"Here you go, Granny," Doug said, sliding the cup toward her.

Granny opened her mouth but said nothing, her chest heaving with effort. She leaned on the counter, lowered her head, and sunk to her knees.

"I can't breathe," she whispered.

The paramedics knew Granny by name. "Hi, Marcella," they said. They asked about her spot on Market Street and if she made much money.

"Enough," she told them.

The paramedics spoke loudly, and Granny protested that she wasn't deaf. They tugged on plastic gloves and peeled back her coat and layers of sweaters and T-shirts and listened to her heart. They looked through the plastic bags hanging from her wheelchair and examined some pill bottles with prescription labels, including one for heart medication. Granny could not say when she'd taken her last pill. The paramedics made some notes on a chart and asked her age. Seventy-eight, Granny said. They loaded her on a gurney.

Granny protested, worried about her dog. I asked Terry, a floor supervisor, to call around and find a kennel where we could board her until Granny was released. Terry picked up the dog and went to lock her in a back room.

"She has lice," a paramedic whispered to me but loud enough for Terry to hear, and she dropped the dog, which yelped and ran behind the wheelchair and peed.

"Jesus!" Granny gasped. "What are you doing to Missy?"

"Not the dog," the paramedic said. "*Granny* has lice. Head lice."

I looked at Granny, who was holding her cap in her hands, gray, sweat-dampened hair plastered to her forehead. She made a face as the paramedics wheeled her out.

Terry found a kennel and asked Poppa Ron to take the dog there. Terry had been at the center about a year. She was short and stocky and wore a fatigue jacket and military-style boots. When she wasn't talking, her mouth settled into a perpetual frown. During staff meetings, she would cross her arms and lean back in her chair. She reminded me of one of those inflatable punching bags that always bounces back no matter how many times you knock it down. She said she had been an army nurse and had served in Vietnam, but whenever any of us asked her a health question, no matter how simple, she would refuse to answer. She claimed that, as a retired medical professional, she could be sued if she gave incorrect advice. We took her no more seriously than we did Doug.

Shortly before Granny began coming to the center, Terry had announced that she had stomach cancer. She had not been diagnosed with it; she just knew, she said, because of her medical training. She began seeing doctor after doctor. Each told her she had an upset stomach, nothing more, and recommended an antacid. But then her abdomen began to swell. She wasn't pregnant—not at fifty-eight. A doctor at San Francisco General Hospital ran some tests, and to everyone's surprise she did indeed have stomach cancer.

Terry began getting chemo and lost her hair but continued to work, dying slowly on the job.

Three days later I was in my office talking to Julie, one of my volunteers, when Granny returned from the hospital. A social worker had given her a bus token and referred her to us, recommending that we place her in a homeless shelter. Granny leaned on a cane by the front desk until Doug helped her into the drop-in area. She carried a plastic bag full of medications and had on clean clothes: a white button-down shirt too big for her narrow frame, corduroy pants held up by suspenders, clean sneakers, and a Windbreaker. Her shampooed hair floated about her face. Granny asked for her wheelchair and her dog. Doug yelled to Poppa Ron about picking up the dog, then got the wheelchair from a padlocked closet. Granny sunk into it, exhausted. She stared into a corner with that isn't-this-something look on her face and then closed her eyes. Julie stood up to help, but I waved her back to her seat.

Julie was transgender, over six feet tall, a hulking figure. She often wore a pink blouse, a red skirt, and a pair of scuffed red heels. Old track marks lined her arms and calves, and her weathered, rouged face looked as if she had gone twelve rounds with life and lost. When she spoke, she took cavernous breaths, bringing forth words from somewhere deep within her. Her voice would not sound feminine no matter how hard she tried. She wore a blond wig that slipped off when she was in a hurry, and stray lipstick spotted the stubble on her chin. The day of Granny's return Julie told me she needed to take time off to attend her grandmother's funeral in Jackson, Mississippi. She wondered if the center would help pay for her bus ticket. I told her I'd check our petty-cash fund.

"Are you going to the funeral as Manuel or Julie?" I asked. Manuel was the name her parents had given her, and she used it sometimes.

"I haven't decided," she said. "I'd like to go as the woman I am."

"If I were you," I said, "and I didn't want to be buried with my grandmother, I'd go as Manuel."

"You're not me."

As Julie left my office, I glanced at my watch. Almost five. The center closed in an hour. It had originally operated twenty-four hours a day, seven days a week. Then our funding had been cut. Now we remained open seven days a week but for only nine hours a day. I looked at Granny asleep in her wheelchair, wrapped in her Windbreaker, the rise and fall of her chest barely discernible. Then I stood and looked through her plastic bag and found three pill bottles and a note explaining that the medications were for her heart, blood pressure, and pneumonia. Pneumonia. Outside, a rolling fog descended. I shouted for Poppa Ron to call some homeless shelters.

But all the shelters with beds for women had dealt with Granny before and told Ron they would have nothing to do with her, pneumonia or no. The reasons varied: She insisted on sleeping in her wheelchair. She would not take a shower. She had a dog.

Granny, as Ron would say, was "ass out" of options. We could do nothing more for her. Julie gave her a blanket so she might keep warm on the street at night. I watched her tuck it around Granny's lap. I had turned a lot of homeless men, women, and families away. "We're full," I'd explain, or, "We're closed now. Here's a blanket. Here're a couple of sandwiches. Come back tomorrow." I had always been able to shut down a part of myself and rationalize that I had no other choice, that I could do only so much.

However, I couldn't justify throwing Granny out. Not an old woman with a bad heart who a few days earlier had looked as if she might die in front of us. No shelter would accept her because she insisted on some measure of independence. Difficult as Granny could be, I found in her stubbornness something life-affirming and admirable, and worthy of effort on her behalf.

I stared out the window at an abandoned car and a homeless guy talking animatedly to a parking meter. The owner of a burger joint across the street was standing in his doorway, sipping a Coke. When he'd first opened, he had allowed my staff and volunteers to charge their lunches. I don't know how much money he lost before he wised up and became a cash-only business and my staff went back to the soup lines and raiding the center's canned-goods donation closet—until I put a lock on it. I listened to the whistling wheeze of Granny's breathing. The evening light, filtered by fog, shaded the planes of her cheekbones, the sunken hollows of her jaw. I turned back to Ron and told him we'd put Granny up at the center.

"Here?" Ron said. "She can't be here alone."

"I'll stay tonight."

"And tomorrow?"

"We'll figure out tomorrow, tomorrow," I said.

I told Granny I insisted on certain conditions. In exchange for staying at the center, she would need to use her Social Security check to rent a room or a small apartment instead of blowing it on storage lockers. There were places with subsidized units she could afford. I would help her empty the lockers. In addition, Granny would work at the front desk every morning, signing people in who needed to see our benefits advocate. "You have to earn your keep," I said. Granny imitated my stern look and then laughed, her face crinkling into dozens of lines. I told her I'd pair her with Napalm at the front desk, and she stopped laughing.

Ron shut off the lights except the ones in the drop-in, where Granny would spend the night in her wheelchair. I would sleep in my office. But first I ran across the street and bought two hamburgers, an order of fries, and two Cokes. When I returned, Ron got up to leave.

"No fooling around," he said, and grinned.

"Don't forget to pick up the damn dog," I told him, and I locked the door behind him.

Granny and I sat at the counter and ate. She thanked me for the burger and asked where in San Francisco I lived. I told her I didn't live in the city; I rented a house on a hill overlooking vineyards in Sonoma County. Some neighbors raised horses, and one had sheep that he let into his house. Granny made a face. She popped a fry into her mouth and said she'd grown up on a farm. Her family had kept chickens. I told her my mother had raised chickens when she was a girl, and my older brother had once had a pet duck named Quacker. "A duck is not a chicken," Granny said. "Thank you," I said. She told me her childhood home had stood where the Civic Center Plaza was now, and that she was a member of *the* Brooks family for whom the exhibition center Brooks Hall was named. She'd been specially invited to attend the grand opening.

I asked what it was like.

"Crowded."

"Who was there?"

"All the famous people of the city."

"Like who?"

"All of them," Granny said.

"When did it open?"

"Years ago."

I stopped asking questions. We finished our burgers and fries, and I went to my office. I didn't believe Granny was related to the Brooks family any more than I was. Then again, I hadn't believed Terry had cancer.

In the morning Granny had coffee, and Paul brought her a breakfast of toast and oatmeal from Saint Anthony's Soup Kitchen. She sat at the front desk, and when we opened, she told the stream of people pushing through the door to "Sign in, goddamn it." When the initial rush was over, I asked Granny to show me her storage lockers.

She rented three on Turk Street and one off Van Ness Avenue. I suggested we check out the Van Ness locker first. We walked several blocks to get there, Granny pausing from time to time to catch her breath, leaning heavily on her wheelchair.

When we opened the Van Ness locker, I saw a kitchen table set with plates and silverware and a yellow rug beneath it. Boxes filled with tissue-wrapped cups and glasses and cutting boards were stacked against the concrete walls. Sheets covered a red mohair sofa and a gray lounge chair. Some of the furniture, Granny said, had belonged to her parents. Some of it she had bought when she'd cleaned houses in Pacific Heights.

Granny and I spent another night at the center, and the following day we walked to the Turk Street lockers. These were filled with boxes of old newspapers, magazines, rusted cans, broken pieces of furniture, and frayed clothes, some green with mold and looking as if they'd been pulled from a dumpster. At first I thought the newspapers and magazines might have stories about the Brooks family, but I found only dead mice between the gnawed pages. It was as if there were two Grannys: the methodical, organized woman on Van Ness, and the bag lady on Turk.

I started clearing the Turk Street lockers, since they appeared to contain nothing of value. I wore a scarf around my face and filled garbage bags. Granny wrung her arthritic hands as I discarded one pile of magazines after another, her face wrinkled with worry. Finally, she couldn't stand it. When I took a break, she started emptying the bags back into the lockers.

"Granny! What are you doing?"

"Ooh," she said, reaching into a bag to withdraw a wrinkled *Life* magazine between her thumb and forefinger as if it were a gold nugget. "Can't get rid of this. No, no."

"Why not?"

"This is very old," she said appraising the magazine with a cocked brow and then placing it deliberately in the locker, careful to disturb only cobwebs.

I gave up on clearing the lockers that day and suggested she consolidate, moving a load of things she felt she had to keep to the Van Ness locker. Granny agreed. But the torn magazines and other odds and ends did not fit with the dollhouse tranquility on Van Ness. Without any urging from me, Granny discarded the items we had piled in her wheelchair and pushed over from Turk Street. She looked morosely at the trash bins spilling over with her garbage. I asked Granny what she was thinking.

"Nothing," she said. "I'm tired."

Sometimes Granny and I walked to a small restaurant on Golden Gate Avenue for lunch. The owner was obsessed with salads. He screamed "Salad!" when we walked through the door and brought us two whether we wanted them or not. In addition to the salads, I ordered two BLTs. Granny asked for a glass of red wine. She watched a waiter pour it, and then she sipped it, her pinkie in the air. She closed her eyes, tipped her head back, and swallowed. I could tell that she had left me for a memory. I never asked where she disappeared.

After lunch I walked Granny back to the center and then left to attend meetings. Whenever I was gone longer than Granny preferred, guys on the street would tell me, "Your grandmother is looking for you," and laugh. When I'd get back and ask Granny what she needed, she'd have little to say other than that she had cleaned my office or had put a quarter in the parking meter, saving me from a ticket. Sometimes, as I was leaving the center, she would shout my name. If I was in a hurry I'd say, "Not now, Granny, not now," but she would continue calling "Malcolm!" her voice cracking and then getting louder, "Malcolm!" primordial in its insistence, its need.

At night Granny and I sat in the drop-in and listened to the windows trembling from the trucks rumbling past and watched the shadows roam across the walls. We rarely spoke. I'd hear water drip somewhere, the creaking of pipes. Men and women drifted by outside shrouded in fog, hazy reflections of who they had been during the day. I felt the solace of the empty building, released from the echoing demands of needy people.

One night I cracked open a can of beer I had bought at a corner store.

"What's that?" Granny asked.

"Beer."

"Why?"

"Because I'm thirty-five and single and spending my nights with a seventy-eight-year-old woman."

Granny got a kick out of that.

Once I asked if she'd ever married. "Oh, I had plenty of boys," she said. "Went out with one in the afternoon, another at night."

"But were you ever married?"

She shrugged. I let it go and watched her begin to fall asleep, the dog curled on her lap.

"Where'd you get Missy?"

Granny opened one eye and rolled her head toward me. "Found her," she said, and then she closed her eye, keeping any further information to herself.

About a month after Granny began staying at the center, Terry requested a vacation. She said she had family in Florida she wanted to visit. She had no vacation time coming, but I gave it to her because I sensed what lay behind her request. She left on a Wednesday, just after our weekly staff meeting, which she attended in a wheelchair with a brown suitcase at her side. The chemo had shrunk the stomach tumor, and Terry too. Her clothes hung loosely, and her skin looked ashen. She wore a red beret to conceal the bald patches on her head.

I went over schedules, shift changes, budget reports. When I'd finished, I asked if anyone had anything they wanted to bring up. Terry raised her hand and withdrew a sheet of paper from her pocket. Unfolding it, she read our names and what she liked about each of us. She included some gentle criticism: Poppa Ron was too nice and allowed participants to take advantage of him. I attended too many meetings. Doug should brew stronger coffee. Granny needed to bathe her damn dog. Then Terry folded her list and put it back in her pocket.

"That's all I have to say," she said. "I'm leaving for Florida."

We stood up and one by one hugged her.

Poppa Ron drove Terry to the airport. She died in Tampa three weeks later.

I remained with Granny overnight at the center for eight weeks. During that time, she finished emptying all three of her Turk Street lockers. I helped her put the money she saved into a bank account, and we began filling out housing applications. Sometimes Poppa Ron spared me and spent the night with Granny, and sometimes Julie did. Tommy, one of my counselors, filled in too. He was an easygoing, beefy guy with a rambunctious laugh and a clownish sense of humor. He worked the front desk alongside Granny in the morning and called her "Miss Marcella." Beneath his humor, however, was a paranoia that made him question the motivation behind any kindness. He was convinced that I was helping Granny clear her lockers only because they held objects of value. My nights with her, he thought, were interrogation sessions during which I tried to get her to relinquish her treasures to me. I told him I was more than happy to let him take over and help Granny empty her lockers. He returned to the center one afternoon holding a wooden coffee grinder that Granny had given him. She said it had belonged to her mother. After work Tommy caught a bus to a Mission District antique store and sold it for fifteen dollars. The next morning, he showed me the receipt from the sale.

"I got mines," he said.

The newly opened Turk Street Apartments had several government-subsidized units available. I met with the landlord, who put Granny on his waiting list. About four weeks later he called and offered her a studio apartment. Her rent would be just six hundred

a month. I sat with Granny as she signed the forms. Poppa Ron
picked up her furniture from the Van Ness locker and delivered it
to her new place. I visited the next day and was impressed at how
quickly she had arranged her living space. Plates and cups filled the
kitchen cupboards. The sofa stood against one wall on blue carpet-
ing. The round breakfast table and four chairs took up a corner.
Sunlight filled the room and illuminated a painting of a red barn
that Granny had hung on the newly painted white walls. Missy
stood on a deck overlooking Turk Street and barked at the pigeons.
Granny wore a bright yellow dress, a white apron around her waist.

I told her I was proud of her.

"Shoo," she said, and blushed.

The following morning Granny walked into the center pushing
her wheelchair and wearing a fur coat, rouge on her cheeks, and
eye makeup. She took off her coat and threw it at me, then laughed
at my astonished look. She kicked up one leg to show off her high
heels and then reached for her wheelchair to stop from falling.

"Lord, what having a home can do to some people!" Julie
shouted.

A week later in January 1992, Julie left for Mississippi as Manuel.
She called once to tell me the funeral was beautiful, "but, Malcolm,
I forgot how hot Mississippi can be!" She had met a wonderful man,
"a big ol' bear of a man, Malcolm!" at the reception afterward. She
didn't elaborate, didn't call again, and didn't return to San Francisco.

My father called me at the center about that time to tell me my
Uncle Joe had died after a long illness. He was eighty. After I got
off the phone, I walked around the block to shake off the shock. I
remembered how Joe had helped me when I lived in New York and
the dinners I'd shared with him. I wrestled with the regret of not
having kept in touch. I must have mentioned my bad news to someone on my way out, because when I returned, Granny said, "I heard
about your uncle. I just want you to know I know." She reached for

my hand. "I want to give you this." And she wrapped her hands around mine.

That was it. But it was enough.

Three months after she moved into the Turk Street Apartments, Granny again began amassing what I can only describe as garbage: discarded newspapers and magazines, pieces of broken metal, wooden boards, even twigs. Someone had given her two cats. She also had two pigeons that she kept in cages she never cleaned. Circular stains began to mar the blue carpet. The apartment reeked of cat piss and body odor, and Granny kept the thermostat on high, exacerbating the stench. She would not let me or anyone else clean her place and bustled around in a frenzy at the mere suggestion: "Don't touch anything! Don't touch anything!" Other tenants began complaining. Granny said people needed to mind their own goddamn business. When I suggested that her neighbors had reason to be concerned, she told me to shut the hell up. She stopped paying rent and began staying in her old spot on Market Street. The landlord tossed her furniture and charged the center a thousand-dollar cleaning fee. I released the pigeons and kept the cats.

Granny continued coming into the center for coffee, wearing several layers of clothes and smelling of wood smoke from the homeless encampment where she spent her nights. She drank her coffee and then made her way to Market Street, avoiding me.

One afternoon I saw two paramedics attending to her and asked what was wrong. Someone had called 911 about an old woman in a wheelchair who appeared dead, they told me. "I was asleep," Granny said. But she appeared to be having trouble breathing, and the paramedics put an oxygen mask over her nose and mouth and told her they wanted her examined at San Francisco General Hospital.

"She has lice," they said. "Do you know her?"

I did, I said, and told them where I worked.

"C'mon, Marcella," they said.

I took Missy.

Granny remained in the hospital for seven days. She had suffered a mild heart attack. I visited her one afternoon. She was as pale as her white hospital gown and complained about the food. I went across the street and bought her some spaghetti at an Italian restaurant. She twined the noodles around a plastic fork, spattering her chin with red sauce. "Why can't the hospital serve food like this?" she wanted to know. Her gown drooped off her right shoulder, and I noticed a large tattoo snaking down her spine. Granny saw me looking at it and pulled up her gown.

"Got that in the navy," she said, her mouth full of spaghetti. "Dubya-dubya two. Australia. With MacArthur."

"Wasn't that the Philippines?"

"He came to Australia after the Philippines," she said. "Terowie."

"What?"

"Terowie."

I stopped at the library on my way back to the center and looked through histories of World War II. Women, I learned, did serve in the navy then and called themselves WAVES, short for Women Accepted for Volunteer Emergency Service. And General Douglas MacArthur, after being forced out of the Philippines by the Japanese in early 1942, had ended up in Australia. It was in the small town of Terowie that he made his "I shall return" speech.

I left the library no more certain about Granny than when I had entered. She could have heard about Terowie in any number of places. And she could have been in the WAVES too. In the end it didn't matter whether she was speaking the truth or making up stories. I'd still be looking after her when she was discharged from the hospital.

And, sure enough, another hospital social worker gave Granny another bus token, and she walked into the center with another note recommending we find her shelter. She was smaller and gaunter than I remembered. I told her she could stay at the center until we found her another place to live. The same rules applied: She would have to volunteer. In addition, when she got a new apartment, someone from the center would help her maintain it, and that would mean tossing anything she brought in from the street. Granny agreed. I fully expected a replay of what we had just been through, but I had no idea what else to do. Despite her contrary nature, I had become very fond of Granny. The mysteries of her life intrigued me. She might sabotage all my best efforts on her behalf but I could not abandon her. The center was meant for people like Granny.

"You're killing me," I told her.

"Shoo," she said. "I'm your ticket into heaven."

We found Granny a room in a government-subsidized residential hotel not far from the center. The twelve-by-twelve-foot space held nothing more than a bed, dresser, closet, and mirror. Poppa Ron, Tommy, Doug, and I visited Granny regularly and threw away newspapers and magazines and anything else that began to accumulate. I expected Granny to object, but she was strangely passive and watched us scour her room without complaint. "Well, here I am," she would say, that isn't-this-something look on her face. She used an inhaler now, and her breath rattled in her chest. She stopped coming into the center except for one afternoon to tell me that Missy had died. I walked with her back to her room and found the dog stretched out on the floor. Rigor mortis had begun to set in. Granny knelt beside Missy, balled her hands in the dog's fur, and wept. I had questioned much of what Granny had told me about her life, but I had no doubt about her sorrow. When she stood, I wrapped Missy in a towel and told Granny I would bury her. On the way out, I noticed a cracked metal bucket filled with dirt, twigs, and feathers that had spilled across some yellowed newspapers. I cleaned it all up and carried it out with Missy.

Two months afterward, on a warm June afternoon brushed by breezes off the bay, Tommy discovered Granny dead in her room, seated in her wheelchair, head drooped to one side, eyes closed, and a blanket across her lap. The hoarded secrets of her life were hers forever now. A box in Granny's closet held her birth certificate, a high-school diploma, and a yellowed black-and-white photo of a young woman who looked very much like her. According to the birth certificate, Granny was ninety, not seventy-eight, as she'd told us. But her name was Marcella Brooks.

I spoke with the San Francisco Coroner's Office about burying her, but since neither I nor anyone else at the center was related to Granny, her body could not be released to us. Instead it would be held for twelve months. If no family member claimed it, the body would be cremated and the ashes scattered. A priest, the coroner said, would be present.

The year Granny died, 1994, I left the center to run a Sonoma County program for undocumented day laborers. Months passed, then a year. Then three. I never saw Tommy again. Poppa Ron died of lung cancer. Doug and Paul left for the Midwest, where they had family. In 1997 I accepted a job in Philadelphia. The center remained in the Tenderloin but was relocated to a larger building. Strict new rules required people seeking help to develop a "stabilization plan." They had to be actively trying to find a job and a place to live, or they'd be expelled from the program.

On my last day of work in Sonoma County, I saw an elderly, stoop-shouldered woman sorting through discarded bottles and cans by the side of the road and tossing them into a plastic garbage bag she dragged behind her. For no good reason I stopped what I was doing, went outside, and joined her. I picked up a bottle and dropped it in her bag. She heard it clink against the other bottles.

"Oh," she said, her eyes wide, delighted.

She continued searching the ground. I walked beside her. Her lips moved, forming silent words I was unable to decipher. She took furtive glances at me, as if I made her uncomfortable. I offered her another dirt-encrusted bottle. She reached for it, and we held it between us. Her mouth twitched and she muttered words I did not understand before she put it into her bag and hurried away.

Eastbound

(1997)

BAR, the sign read. I went inside.

NOW SERVING TAMMY AND MONICA, I read on a chalk-board by the restroom. I paused, sat down, ordered a beer, and put three dollars on the bar.

"Ten bucks," the bartender said.

I looked at him, my eyes wide.

"Whorehouse prices," he said.

He opened a refrigerator and took out a can of Budweiser, snapped off the tab, and set the can on a napkin. He gave me a tall glass dripping with water. I saw a note on the mirror behind the bar reminding patrons to use condoms. I put a twenty-dollar bill by my glass and wiped sweat off my forehead. A ceiling fan turned above me, but the air didn't move.

"I'll call Tammy," the bartender said. "You'll like her. Monica's busy."

"I don't want a girl. Just the beer. I didn't know. I mean, there's no sign about, you know, what you do here."

"We're called The Hotel California," the bartender said, and pointed to some T-shirts on the wall bearing the name. "This is Nevada, man. It's not illegal."

"I know, but it just said 'bar' outside."

"Got you in here, didn't it?"

He rang up my beer and gave me the change. A big man with a red beard walked in, followed by a woman carrying a bag of groceries. She set the bag on the bar and the bartender peered inside.

"Thanks for taking Monica to the store," he said to Red Beard.

"She owes me," Red Beard told him. "I've run her around more than enough for you today. I expect a free one."

"What are you talking about?" Monica said.

"You heard me. I get a free one. Gas costs money."

Monica rolled her eyes. Her face was parchment tight, mouth thin. Her breasts pushed out against her small white T-shirt but there was nothing enticing about the display. She lit a cigarette, took a drag, and held it before releasing her breath in one long exhalation that tightened her face even more.

I sipped my beer. I had driven eight hours eastbound on Interstate 80 from San Francisco before I stopped for the night here in Elko. I was on my way to Philadelphia. I figured it would take me four more eight-hour days to get there. I'd checked into a motel. From my room I saw the bar sign a few blocks away and decided to have a cold one.

I had spent the previous night with Sandy, my ex. We'd never married but had been together for eight years, six of those under one roof. All sorts of reasons for our split. If I were to settle on *the* reason, the one neither of us wanted to articulate as we refused to compromise on our differences, it would be that we had stopped loving each other the way we needed to if we were to spend the rest of our lives together. The drifting apart had happened gradually. When we finally noticed, we were at a loss to stop it. However, we still loved each other in our way.

A year after Sandy and I separated, I accepted a job at the *Philadelphia Inquirer*. At thirty-nine and after having lived in San Francisco for fourteen years, I was starting over.

Sandy was stunned when I told her about the *Inquirer* job. Despite our split, we would get together from time to time, not to reconcile but to ease into living alone. My move to Philadelphia would end the transition period.

"When do you leave?" she asked.

"Next week."

"Next week!"

Pause.

"Will you come see me before you go?"

"I want to," I said.

A woman in a thin satin robe with a purple flower motif walked out of a room behind the bar and sat beside me. I could see her black bra, flat stomach, and black panties through the robe. Her black hair fell to her shoulders and her blue eyes were wide and hesitant. She wore just enough makeup to highlight her cheeks. Small furrows descended from her mouth, giving the impression of a pout. She wasn't hard like Monica, but I could see the hardness coming.

"This is Tammy," the bartender said.

He turned to her. "He thought we were just a bar. He just wants his beer. I told him you'd be more interesting to talk to than me."

"Oh," Tammy said. "You don't want a girl?"

"No."

"Ask him to buy you a glass of wine at least," Monica chimed in. "Don't give him your time for nothing."

"Right," Tammy said. "Would you buy me a glass of wine?"

"If you get her wine or a drink she gets half the bar tab," the bartender said.

"Okay."

"Five bucks."

I put five dollars on the bar and the bartender poured a glass of red wine. He put two-fifty in a tip jar for Tammy.

"I had a real nice guy the other night," Tammy told Monica. "He said he'd take me to a movie."

"A date?"

"Yeah. He's going to stop here sometime tonight and then we'll go out."

Tammy turned to me and asked what I was doing in Elko. On my way to Philadelphia, I told her. She said she would be flying to New York City in a few months to meet with representatives of the United Nations. Her mother was Iranian, Tammy explained. She believed she was owed thousands of dollars from Iranian assets frozen by the US government since 1979, when Americans were taken hostage in Tehran.

"That money belongs to all Iranians," she said. "When I'm paid I'm going to travel the world and then run my own business."

I didn't say anything. Tammy had not decided what sort of business she wanted to start. She said she had been a Realtor before the bottom fell out of Nevada real estate. Four weeks ago, she started working here. She would return to real estate when the market picked up.

"He saved my life," she said of the bartender. "He gave me a job."

This morning I had gotten up early. I dressed and carried my duffel bag to my car. When I came back inside, Sandy was sitting on the black couch she'd bought without asking me and that had caused one of our countless arguments.

"Coffee?" she asked.

"I'm good, thanks."

"I'll visit you in Philadelphia," she said.

"Christmas."

"That would be good, yes."

"We always enjoyed Christmas together," I said.

We hugged. Both of us gave in to choked sobs. Then I walked outside to my car. I waved; Sandy raised an arm. I drove around the block and stopped in front of the house, hoping she would still be standing there, but the front door was closed.

"Would you like me to show you around?' Tammy asked.

"Okay," I said.

"I'm ready for that free one," Red Beard said.

"Shut up," Monica said. "Last time I ask a favor from you."

I followed Tammy into a room with a cot and a couch. A hot tub stood in a corner. I smelled the wet heat rising from the tub.

"This room is used for parties," Tammy said.

She didn't elaborate. She sat on the cot and watched me. The robe sagged open around her breasts. I looked away.

"What else?" I asked.

She got up and led me out of the room and down a hall, opening a door that had her name on it. A bed with a white comforter was pressed against the wall near an open closet. Skirts and blue jeans hung on hangers. An ironing board leaned against a wall. A McDonald's plastic cup half filled with soda stood on a dresser.

"We're charged thirty dollars a day to live here," Tammy said.

"Steep."

"That's why I like doing parties. You can make a thousand dollars with one party. The house keeps half. That's still five hundred for me."

She stopped talking and loosened her robe.

"It's been slow this week," she said, facing me. "Depending on what you want, I could probably give it to you cheap. I'd have to ask, though."

I felt my face turn red. If Sandy saw me now: *Sure, you didn't know it was a brothel.* I could just hear her. I smiled at the thought. Tammy smiled back. I shook my head.

"No," I said. "I really only wanted a beer. I just saw the sign outside and came in."

"Oh." She tightened her robe. "Buy me another wine, then."

"Sorry?"

"Would you buy me another wine? So I can make a little cigarette money off you at least?"

"Of course," I said.

After I'd left Sandy, I drove into downtown San Francisco and drifted through North Beach. I passed a bagel shop she and I had often stopped at for breakfast. I continued on to City Lights Bookstore, where we sometimes went to browse on Saturdays. I took Clay Street to I-80. Within two hours I'd reached Sacramento and continued on to Lake Tahoe. Then came the California-Nevada border. I pulled in to a rest stop and stared at the interstate, its long gray lanes stretching east to the horizon. I can always turn back, I reminded myself. I can always turn back.

Tammy and I sat back down at the bar. I ordered a glass of wine and a beer.

"Nothing?" the bartender asked, looking at Tammy and then at me.

"Nothing," Tammy said and sipped her wine.

"Well," the bartender said to me, "you *did* say you only wanted a beer."

He dropped another two-fifty in the jar for Tammy. I concentrated on my beer. Red Beard took Monica by the arm.

"C'mon," he said.

"Let go!" she snapped.

"Stop it!" the bartender said and slapped the bar with his palm. "Christ, I gave you a drink. How much longer you going to go on about a free one for some goddamn groceries? You've been coming in here too long to act the fool."

Red Beard dropped Monica's arm.

"You owe me," he said, jabbing a finger at the bartender. "Gas money."

As he stormed out the door a sharp splash of sunlight burst into the bar. For seconds I couldn't see. I blinked, heard a truck start. The bartender blurred into view and I watched him freshen Monica's drink. She carried it down the hall, her face etched in shadow against the wall. The truck pulled away.

"I never thought I'd be doing this," Tammy whispered to me.

Her warm breath washed against my ear, and she placed a hand on my knee. I turned to her. She seemed very slight and small. I knew she didn't believe a word she had said about the UN and frozen Iranian assets. I knew she had no experience in real estate. I knew her customer from the other night didn't exist, or if he did, he would never take her to a movie. I knew her name wasn't Tammy.

I also knew that I had left San Francisco for good. I had days of hard driving ahead, and when I reached Philadelphia, Sandy would not visit me at Christmas.

I finished my beer and told Tammy it had been a pleasure meeting her. She bounced back with a chirpy request for me to remember her because we might see each other again. After all, Philadelphia was not that far from New York City, was it?

"No, it's not," I said.

I got in my car and drove down the street to my motel room. I opened the door to the empty bed and dusty chest of drawers and the thin light filtering through the faded curtains. I stepped inside and closed the door. In the musty silence, I whispered, "Good-bye."

Good-bye.

Good-bye.

I felt the words come off my tongue and leave my mouth and dissolve into the quiet. I stretched out on the bed and stared at the ceiling. The morning would be the start of another long day. I closed my eyes and tried to sleep.

My Middle Age

(2003)

Jet lag. I've been back from Afghanistan three days but still I can't sleep. Gone five months, my third trip there. I'd have thought I'd be used to the travel by now. I look at the clock. Four a.m. I look out my bedroom window at the Kansas City skyline. It would be about noon in Kabul. I kick out of bed, call my dogs. The white one looks up bleary-eyed from the floor. The black one's somewhere. I can't see him, but I hear the ID tag rattle on his collar. I flip on a light.

"Walk," I say.

Before we go outside I push aside maps of Honduras for a reporting trip I'm planning and open my laptop to check email. The computer makes a popping sound, and a little bubble rises in the lower right-hand corner. I have one message and click on it.

Tom is dead.

The sender, my childhood friend Gabrielle, had dated Tom in high school and remained fond of him despite the passage of years, changes in geography, marriage, and children. I suppose she just needed to blurt out her shock and grief in the way we do things now: tweets, email, Facebook, texting. No more the assurance of a sympathetic voice on the other end of a phone to convey the bad news.

Tom is dead.

I hadn't heard from him in years. I would call him, but he never answered and did not have voice mail so I could leave a message.

Eventually his phone was disconnected. I mentioned Tom to Gabrielle in an email from Kabul while I was stuck in the airport on my way home. I had seen some kids playing soccer and thought of him. I didn't know it at the time, but after Gabrielle received my message, she searched the Internet and found a one-paragraph news brief that said Tom had been found dead in his Dallas apartment.

The brief stated that Tom was forty-six years old. It did not suggest foul play. The last time I had spoken to him by phone, he had just been released from a psych ward for attempted suicide. Pills and vodka. Just got drunk and stupid, he said, embarrassed to have been locked up with people "who had real problems."

I sit down, weighted with sleeplessness, and try to wrap my head around Gabrielle's message.

Tom is dead.

1982

I am sitting in the living room of Tom's future brother-in-law Brad in Winnetka, Illinois. He has just returned from Afghanistan, backpacking in a war zone. Dig it. Brad's a rangy kind of guy: tall, lean, sandy hair. Confident. He describes the occupation of Kabul by Soviet troops. Soldiers on every corner. Afghans hustling past them, avoiding eye contact.

I tell him I'd like to go there. I'm itching for something. College grad, working the stockroom of a Crate & Barrel in Skokie. Former English major filled with stories of the Left Bank and Hemingway and how all the writers of that time traveled the world and witnessed history: World War I, Spanish Civil War, World War II. I was also taken by Jack Kerouac and his manic road trips across America with Neal Cassady.

Now here's this guy, Brad, sitting in front of me on a white couch, living the adventuresome life I imagine for myself. Laura, Tom's girlfriend and future wife, sits beside her brother, smiling.

Proud. She designs window displays at Crate & Barrel. Tom works there too. He got me my job. I also write feature stories for Lerner Newspapers, a suburban chain.

"I can give you contacts in Afghanistan if you're serious," Brad tells me.

"Sure," I say.

I know I won't go. Still, it's fun to pretend and pretend I'm not pretending. I'm twenty-five and live with my parents. I need to get out. Get out like Brad. Like Tom. He and Laura share a Chicago apartment. I don't want to think about what I'm going to do. It seems so complicated. Right now, I'll settle for pretending I'm going to Afghanistan.

In the morning I'll be back in the Crate & Barrel stockroom. Barely into my twenties and I feel left behind in my own life.

"He'll go to Afghanistan," Tom tells Brad. "He'll do it."

Tom has complete faith in me. He'll go, he says again in that voice of his that rises and cracks in a kind of joyful agitation whenever he gets excited. The same voice that shouted encouragement to his teammates on our high school soccer team. He was one of the best players in the state then, and his future in sports seemed assured.

2001

I am leaving for Afghanistan two months after September 11. I have twenty-four hours to get ready. I am a reporter at the *Kansas City Star*. Flyover country, but even the *Star* is sending people to Afghanistan. A beat reporter's moment. My heart races. I call my parents.

"They can't just send you like that, you have to prepare," my father blusters on the phone. I laugh, can't believe I'm going.

I don't think of Tom and our evening in his brother-in-law's apartment nearly twenty years ago. I'm too hyped up to think of anything. When I do think of Tom, six weeks later, I am in Kabul. I call him on a satellite phone but he doesn't answer.

2003

Tom is dead.

Gabrielle's email tells me that Tom died on December 21, 2001, about six weeks after I arrived in Afghanistan.

I shut off my computer and jog down a flight of stairs with my dogs to the door and open it to the sidewalk. A late January snow crunches underfoot, and the dogs leap into piles plowed against the curb and I tug them away from where other dogs have peed, covering my face from a blast of frigid wind blowing off Summit Street. I still see deserts and patrolling US soldiers and men in turbans. My twenty-seven-hour flight from Kabul took me away from Afghanistan faster than I can get it out of my head.

What would I be doing in Kabul now? Having lunch. A little place my colleague Aziz and I always go. I see us sitting on carpets strewn across the floor. We order rice, beans, and cuts of lamb. A waiter tosses water on exposed areas around the rugs to keep dust from rising while we eat. The water spatters my shoes, and I hold out my hands and he pours water over our fingers to clean them. I shake my hands and resume eating. After lunch Aziz and I walk through a hovel of vendor stalls on Butchery Street, where the skinned carcasses of goats and sheep drip blood and crowds of men wrapped in blankets clog the sidewalks. Cars swerve past us, and we make our way amid the raucous beeping and the hundreds of disembodied voices rising around us, and the bustle of shepherds herding goats and mules pulling carts, and the men and women stepping through the debris of bombed buildings, and the kids playing soccer where buildings once stood.

The dogs tug me forward. I enjoy their quiet company. I'm glad to be home, but I haven't called friends. I want to be alone. To ease back into life here before I leave for Honduras. I spend my days in coffee shops, reading newspapers and magazines surrounded by people I don't know, my face buried in articles. I'm in the company of strangers, alone but not alone, and I find comfort in the bubble I've created. But life intrudes. Tom is dead.

If Tom were alive, he'd listen and not ask questions, just let me blab on about how I have a tough time adapting back to Kansas City. Reentry, reporters call it, I'd say, and he'd make a face at that bit of jargon. Oh, is that what they call it, Mr. Whoop-Dee-Do foreign correspondent man, he'd say, is it really, and we'd both laugh.

I wonder if he would remember the evening with Laura's brother. We stayed up late that night and drank too much beer and the next day Tom called me from work and said he hoped I had the same pounding headache he had. Tom began working at Crate & Barrel right after college. Like me, he unloaded trucks and organized a warehouse. His hands and forearms got strong from days spent ripping open fifty-pound box after fifty-pound box of pots and pans.

Unlike me, Tom enjoyed his job and had no desire to be anything other than a Crate & Barrel warehouse supervisor. Laura wanted to establish her own design business. She thought Tom lacked ambition, and that, he told me years later, contributed to problems in their marriage. They divorced in 1994.

Laura had not known Tom in high school when he excelled at soccer and was ranked eighth in Illinois. His coach encouraged him to try out for the Olympic team, certain he would make it, but Tom dismissed the idea. Perhaps he thought subjecting his natural talent to the rigors of that sort of competition would render everything he had accomplished insignificant if he failed. Perhaps he was simply happy with what he had done and saw no need to do more.

Tom had a casual manner when he played soccer, sauntering up to the ball as if it were a stray Coke can on the sidewalk that he hadn't quite decided whether to ignore or not. Then he'd kick it. Fueled with an unseen energy, the ball would rocket between the bare legs of opposing players with the kind of streamlined intensity of something immersed in the celebration of its sudden freedom; it would soar waist-high past even more players, and Tom would stare after it as if it were a bird he had just released, a benign, almost humble look on his face expressing appreciation for his small part in its liberation, for the gift he had given an inanimate object, and he'd watch the ball streak past the goalkeeper before being stopped finally by the net, and dropping heavily to the ground. Tom would look almost disappointed as he considered the abrupt stillness that enwrapped the ball like a dead thing, and he'd slump a little, head bowed. He'd shrug off the backslapping of his teammates and at halftime sit by himself on the bench. After the game he'd seek me out. We'd get in his car and usually stop somewhere for pizza. I would tell him he'd done a great job, and he would say, "Yeah, it was a good game," and nothing more.

One night as we ate pizza, he told me his older sister Kathy had died. "I can't tell you what happened," Tom said. "I can't tell you how she died. Don't ask."

I didn't. Kathy was seven years older than me. I'd barely known her.

At his house, photographs of Kathy had been removed from the walls. Maybe Tom saw me looking at the blank spaces, I don't know, but for no reason he told me his parents had begun sleeping in separate bedrooms. I was eighteen. I didn't know what to say. I think now that Tom wanted desperately to talk about it.

Years later he told me Kathy had committed suicide. Carbon monoxide. She had sat in her car in the garage. She had a history of depression. After the funeral, Tom's father told him to stop crying.

"It's over. We have to continue with our lives," he'd said.

Tom wasn't home when Kathy's photos were removed. He didn't know when or why his parents decided to live detached from each other but remain in the same house. They never mentioned Kathy again.

My dogs keep pulling me. I see their breath and lean back to slow them. I should take them to a training class. There are a hundred and one other things I should do but won't.

I smell the early morning air and the persistent odors of car exhaust, trash, and skunks, and I think of the smell of horses and mules that lingers on Jalalabad Road after dozens of them have hauled wagonloads of wood into Kabul. There is the nauseating stink of horse shit and mule shit mixing with diesel fumes. Mortared buildings stand on either side of the jammed roads, and the homeless inside them stare out holes and watch me take photographs.

Later, I return to the Park Palace Guest House where I'm staying and order kabob. Water leaps out of a fountain in the courtyard, splashing onto the dead grass.

An army contractor joins me. If you're in the shitter, do you think you would finish pissing when a bomb drops? he asks. It's one of those mind-fuck, does-a-falling-tree-make-noise-if-no-one's-around-to-hear-it kind of questions when you've got nothing to do and no place to go, and you've seen all the DVDs you brought with you from the States. Weird thing is, the contractor leaves to take a leak. And I hear a blast from somewhere nearby. Bomb? I doubt it. No commotion on the street to suggest panic but I see the contractor run out of his room. Did he piss himself? Probably not, but the thought makes me laugh.

Walking back to my apartment, I stop outside Los Alamos Market y Cocina, a convenience store across the street. My dogs pant at my side. A breeze rustles the leaves in trees along the sidewalk. Parked cars loom in the dark.

Los Alamos is closed at this early hour, but inside I see the thirty-four-year-old owner, Augustin Juarez, stocking shelves. Brightly lit, Los Alamos reflects Augustin's sunny nature; he is a short, stocky, dark-haired man with an easy grin and a contagious laugh.

One afternoon when I was in the store, he asked to borrow my glasses to better read a purchase order. *Tu está viejo*, I teased him.

You're old. Ever since then, we've always greeted each other, *Hola, viejo!*

Augustin keeps the shelves full and mops the white-tiled floor. Posters of green mountainous valleys shrouded by fat white clouds hang crookedly on the cream-colored walls. People like to drop by and talk even when they have no need to shop. Since I've been back, I've walked into Los Alamos for no particular reason, checking shelves filled with cans of chili, pinto beans, fruit cocktail. I find it oddly comforting to mindlessly pick up cans and put them down and listen to the talk around me without being drawn into it.

KITCHEN OPENING SOON, a sign inside reads. Before I left for Afghanistan, Augustin told me he planned to expand his business by serving Mexican meals that would taste like home cooking. What he earned from the kitchen he would put into a retirement fund. He didn't want to be managing a convenience store when he was a real *hombre viejo*.

I saw Tom for the last time in 1988, when we were both thirty-one. He and Laura had recently moved to Dallas to help open a Crate & Barrel, and I was visiting. We sat in their living room drinking beers and debating the start of middle age while Laura worked in the kitchen, examining designs for the store. I told Tom that if by middle age we meant a halfway mark, then the midpoint of, say, infancy and one hundred would be fifty.

Tom countered that the average life expectancy for men was about seventy-four. Middle age, therefore, would be thirty-seven. Neither of us accepted the idea that middle age was six years away. To be middle-aged at thirty-seven and then three years later turn forty was too much to consider. We stuck with fifty as the midpoint, an age that seemed far into the future.

A dog barks and my dogs' ears prick up. The sound of someone jogging bounces off houses. Streetlights cast a yellow glow, washing out swaths of fading night. I look up at dimming stars and miss the pitch-black skies of Afghanistan.

When I'm in Kabul, I take care in the evening, worried about breaking an ankle in a hole in the sidewalk. Generators hum in some vendors' stalls, and I use the light they provide to make my way. Men and women emerge from the cloudy darkness and walk toward the light to buy rice and bread, and then they walk back into the dark, toward mountains I know are miles away but appear to loom out of the city itself.

"Coco!" boys shout at me, using the Dari word for "uncle," and then they too vanish.

If Tom were here, I'd tell him that everything feels off-kilter when you first arrive in Kabul, and you wonder if you have conjured a kind of skewed dream that you will awaken from soon enough, and then a few weeks later you're used to it and the life around you becomes normal, a new normal, and everything you've known before is really the dream you've awakened from.

I watch Augustin punch buttons on a calculator. Forms from the city health department and a blueprint for the kitchen are spread out on a desk beside him. I can just make out the fine lines of the blueprint. I like the idea of the drawings being transferred from the page and morphing into vents and pipes and plumbing that will all be part of something new.

I don't think of myself as old necessarily, but I'm not young. There is no going back. Tom is frozen in time, just as he was in a favorite high school photograph that hung in his room. The camera had caught him in midair as he jumped up to watch the trajectory of a soccer ball during a game. It looked like he head-butted the ball, but it had in fact been kicked by a teammate. Tom told me he'd jumped because he wanted to see where the ball would land, but I think something else motivated him. What I saw in the photo was a moment of sheer exuberance. Tom couldn't restrain himself and hurled himself into the air, his shoulder-length hair rising off his head, his blue-and-white sports jersey sparkling in the light. It was typical of him that the one photo he had of himself playing the sport he excelled at had nothing to do with him kicking the ball or scoring a point.

Talking about his high school soccer days long after we had graduated did not make him nostalgic or sad. He never regretted passing on the Olympics. He had had his high school moment. He revealed an exceptional talent, then walked away from it, satisfied to open boxes and stock shelves and supervise a warehouse. He would have been interested in my travels, but he would not have understood my restlessness, the worry I have that satisfaction might lead to passivity and that years from now I would look back and regret the risks not taken.

"You don't relax," he'd say. "You're always afraid of what you might miss. You're never satisfied."

I kick a ball of ice and watch it tumble off the sidewalk and break apart. I couldn't play soccer worth a damn. I wonder if Tom had trouble sleeping; if the thing that drove him to take his life kept him up at night until he made a decision. Did he find peace at that point?

I see my life racing forward at an irrevocable clip to this present moment. Time passes. We're either dragged along or keep pace with it. I suspect that at some point Tom felt dragged. He was tired and decided he'd had enough and got off.

A car passes and then another one follows it, and another one after that. The buildup of another workday. Soon the honking congestion of a new morning rush hour will be upon me, but I'll still hear the din of people in Kabul's bazaars and the roving packs of feral dogs howling unseen, see the war widows kneeling on the streets screaming "Money, mister!" and the spreading red blaze of sunrise as mullahs recite the Quran on loudspeakers and call people to prayer.

My dogs pull on their leashes and I look at them and the noises in my head diminish, replaced by the wet hissing sound of the few cars rushing by. The cold air makes my eyes water. There seems to be no end in sight of frigid temperatures, but it's late February and I know spring is not far off. More snow may fall, but winter is almost over.

Tom was born in April. I'll think of him on his birthday. I turn forty-eight in August. However, I tell people I'm that age now. It's a trick I play on myself. When my birthday arrives, I will have already accepted being one year older, worked it in, adjusted to the idea. My birthday will be just another day. I'll have had a jump on time. Tom, I'm sure, would laugh at this self-deception.

A tap on the window startles me, and I see Augustin staring at me. He mouths, *Viejo! Que pasó?*

"*Hola, viejo,*" I say.

He looks confused. Can't sleep? he mouths.

I nod and he shakes his head and returns to his shelves. I cross the street to my apartment, where I hope to fall asleep. I'll dream of Kabul and wake up alone and estranged until I remember where I am. I'll think, Tom is dead, and confront with the steady immutable beat of my heart the loss of a friend, and my own middle age.

Flag Raising

(2004)

From 2000 to 2004, I lived on Summit Street, at 16th Street in the West Side neighborhood of Kansas City, Missouri. One-story wood and brick houses built in the 1940s, curled peels of paint dropping off them like so much falling hair, stood aslant on ruined foundations. Porches that may once have provided romantic interludes for young couples buckled and sagged and held no furniture or any other suggestion of life but only jutted out beneath cracked windows, misshapen and wearied from decades of rain and snow, heat and cold, dimly illuminated by the faint glow of lamps inside.

On the south end of the street, Summit intersected with Southwest Boulevard; on the north side, it came to a dead end above Interstate 70. Feral dogs slept in packs on hills not far from the traffic. In the early morning just before dawn, they would trot down the middle of Summit, the homes on either side of them still dark. Those mornings when I woke up before my alarm clock rang, I would watch the dogs run, seeking cover from the approaching day as streetlights blinked off and a few car engines coughed into life and the sky began to brighten.

The dogs' nights of free roaming, however, would not last. By the time I moved to Summit, developers were already buying up many of the old houses and people like me, with no connection to the neighborhood, began moving in. Changing demographics was nothing new to Summit Street. In the 1880s it had been known as Irish Hill. In subsequent decades, the houses belonged to Swedes, Germans, and Danes, among others. Most of the immigrants worked for the railroads. Mexicans started settling there in large numbers in the 1920s, and it remained largely Mexican when I lived there.

The new promise of rehabbing houses with historic "peaked" gable roofs dating back to the 1870s and increasing property values appealed to developers. Mexican families, however, descendants of relatives who had settled there decades earlier, felt the housing speculation had gotten out of hand. They considered the West Side their ethnic stronghold, the rickety houses were homes to their families, and they couldn't afford the prices—as much as $100,000 in some cases—these rehabbed houses commanded. "I think there's a little clique up there that wants to turn it into Yuppieville, and it's very dangerous," remarked one Hispanic activist, a hairstylist named Alfredo Parra, in an interview with the *Kansas City Star*. "What I see of the West Side is a Chicano community, and I really want us to keep our identity."

Newcomers considered such worries nonsensical. "You have a part of the Mexican population who don't like being integrated," said Kathy Kirby, who was interviewed for the same *Star* story. She had spearheaded neighborhood beautification projects by promoting community gardens. "They won't recognize this has been Northern European in the past, and they don't value an integrated setting."

It did not take me long to see why Mexican families were anxious. Shortly after I arrived, developers built two condominiums on empty lots where houses had been destroyed by fires. The developers promised the mostly Mexican families who attended community meetings that the condos would match in design the style of existing houses and would be only slightly taller. The opposite was true. The condos rose four stories and resembled no other buildings on Summit, each square section a hulking gray cube of modern architecture, each floor placed slightly askew to achieve an effect, I presume, that I did not understand but that a *Star* colleague called "condo cubism."

The deceit of the developers angered me, but I did not feel as violated as the Mexicans who had lived on Summit for generations. I was not raised as a Latino, Chicano, Hispanic. I had no visceral feeling of what those designations meant, no sense of connection to my immigrant forebears or the Spanish-speaking community.

This had to do in part with my father. He was born in St. Louis, Missouri, of Cuban parents. His family later moved to Tampa. Although his first language, he said, was Spanish, I rarely heard him speak it as I was growing up. Every now and then he'd say a word or phrase, but the stumbling sentences emerged with the kind of uncertainty that happens when we evoke a distant memory. If indeed Spanish had been his first language, he lost it growing up. Perhaps in deference to my father, my Puerto Rican mother, who spoke Spanish flawlessly, declined to speak it in the house. My father was not a patient man, and I can't imagine him tolerating my mother talking to his sons in a language he no longer understood.

Spanish was spoken in our house when members of my mother's family visited. At those times, I watched the joy in her face as she spoke, watched the way her hands weaved pictures to accompany her words. Butch, Michael, and I laughed with everyone else, and when the laughter subsided my mother launched into another tale in a rapid-fire tangle of incomprehensible words and rolling *r*s, and the forced tittering of my brothers and me soon became the embarrassed smiles of our ignorance.

On Summit Street, if anyone gave me any thought at all, I presume I was seen as the newcomer I was, one of a group of white trespassers, each of whom had his own plans for the neighborhood but who individually and collectively had no connection to the Mexican community well established there.

With the condos came the enforcement of long-ignored code violations. The *Star* reported that one man whom I'd known as a customer of Los Alamos Market y Cocina, Adolfo Celedon, had sold his house after an enforcement officer cited him for several violations: an overgrown backyard and a leaking roof that heavily damaged the inside of his house. Living on a fixed income and financially strapped, Adolfo told the *Star* he had decided to give up his house and rent a room at the Roslin, a nearby hotel that served indigent people. He was sixty-five and had lived in the neighborhood for fifty years. He had abandoned his two-story brick home for a room with a dresser, an end table, a compact refrigerator, and a toaster oven. A mini TV occupied the one chair beside the big metal bed that dominated the room. Adolfo shared a bathroom down the hall. No shower. A tub only, and a toilet and a sink, and a mirror held together by duct tape. At night a forty-watt bulb illuminated his room. Occasionally I'd see him park his pickup in front of what had been his home, chatting up old friends. Then he vanished.

The people with means liked the neighborhood's economic diversity, Kathy Marchant told the *Star* in the same article. She had moved there in 1982 and opened a restaurant, the Bluebird Bistro, in 1994, described in one advertisement as "eclectic takes on farm-to-table American fare in a renovated, brick-lined Victorian space."

"It's a diverse group of people trying to build something," Marchant said. "It's the healthiest urban environment I've ever lived in. This should be a model for urban redevelopment." She dismissed the word "gentrification" to describe what was happening on the West Side. "That implies, 'We don't care about your life,'" Marchant told the *Star*. "Rich guys moving in on the poor guys. And I don't perceive that happening here."

In my years on Summit, I'd walk to Los Alamos Market most mornings for a cup of coffee. Augustin opened at six except on Sunday and worked until ten at night. His wife and mother helped. A Mexican friend who held three part-time jobs maintained the kitchen. Sometimes Augustin took on side jobs when business was slow. Los

Alamos smelled of steaming pinto beans and melting cheese and the warm aroma of corn tortillas. Bread and canned goods filled warped metal shelves beside other equally overloaded and crooked shelves heavy with cleaning supplies. Two refrigerators packed with soft drinks, fruit juice and milk hummed as loud as radiators. Mariachi music played out of a boom box behind the counter.

One June morning in 2003, as I stood in a line near the counter with Mexican day laborers holding foam cups of black coffee, I noticed a collection jar by the cash register. The men in line put in what change they had.

"What's this?" I asked.

Augustin told me he was raising money for a man found dead in a room below a house on Summit near Southwest Boulevard. The deceased was about five feet six and weighed 130 pounds, according to a one-paragraph news brief in the *Star* Augustin showed me. When the police found him, the body had decomposed so much they had trouble identifying him. He had been dead at least seven days, maybe as many as twelve. Police ruled out homicide. The man who owned the house thought the dead man's name was Enrique Gomez, but he wasn't sure. Augustin thought the name sounded familiar. He had a vague idea of a man he thought might have been Enrique. He hoped people would donate to have him properly buried or sent to family in Mexico.

"Do you recognize the name?" Augustin asked me.

"Enrique?" I shook my head. "No."

Augustin was sure I'd seen him. If Enrique was the man he was remembering, he came into Los Alamos all the time. He was short and skinny, with black hair starting to turn gray. He liked to joke. He was always polite. He let people go ahead of him. Every time Augustin saw him on the street he said hello.

I thought again, but no one came to mind. The next day, thinking that the mystery of Enrique's death might make a good feature story for the *Star*, I walked down Summit to the house where

Augustin said police had found the body. They had been notified by several day laborers who also stayed there that someone had died. I knocked on the door and a short, elderly man looked at me, his face so heavily lined that he could have been chiseled from wood. He took off his glasses and cleaned them on his red denim shirt. I introduced myself and told him I wanted to know about Enrique. I added that I was a regular at Los Alamos.

The old man shook my hand and said his name was Fausto Meixueiro. He had a reputation in the neighborhood for helping migrant workers. He had come to Kansas City from Mexico more than sixty years before and was now eighty-eight. He told me he let homeless Mexicans stay in empty rooms below his house without charge. He looked in on them now and then, but not often. There was nothing in the room worth stealing. He was away when the police had discovered the body.

Fausto also thought the dead man was Enrique Gomez, but he could not swear to it. He thought he had probably known his name at one point, but he never used it and therefore forgot it. He had always called him Caruso, because he liked to sing. Caruso lived with Fausto off and on for about five years. He saved money he earned working on construction sites and in restaurants by depositing it in a savings account Fausto had set up for him. Fausto thought he was working at El Taquito, a tortilla factory in Kansas City, Kansas, when he died. One year, Caruso saved $6,000. He traveled on a train to Mexico through El Paso with all of his money and returned broke three months later.

Fausto patted a worn blue chair, the stuffing blooming out of it like cotton. Enrique used to sit on it some evenings and sing. I looked at the chair and then around the room. Yellowed black-and-white photographs of Fausto's family cluttered two round tables. He revealed that he had divorced some years before, and his eight grandchildren were grown. Stacks of newspapers and magazines filled every space not occupied by furniture. Mildew spangled the walls and dust hung suspended in the still air. A man scuba-dived through clear ocean water on a flat-screen TV.

"I suppose when I die this house will be torn down," Fausto said. "Do you think the memories here will die or remain like ghosts?"

Fausto sank into a chair. He looked small and shrunken. He told me he didn't see Enrique for long periods of time. One day, Enrique left for Chicago for two months. The last time Fausto had seen him, Enrique was walking on Southwest Boulevard. He used to bring Fausto tortillas.

We walked outside and down some broken concrete steps to the dank room where the dead man had been found. I pulled aside an orange curtain and breathed the stale air. A sleeping bag lay crumpled on a damp rug near a refrigerator. Two desks and a small oven stood nearby. Cereal boxes littered the floor.

"I never lived like this," Fausto said.

He gave me a telephone bill and underlined two numbers in Monterrey, Mexico, that the dead man called regularly. I dialed both numbers and listened to the phone ring across the miles. No answer.

"He was a nice man. He would sing, but I didn't know him well," Fausto said. "I miss him. Will you stay and talk?"

"No," I told him. "I need to leave."

He showed me to the door and watched me walk to the sidewalk. Reaching into my pocket for my cell phone, I called El Taquito. The receptionist connected me to the owner, Mike Casey. He had heard about the dead man from police investigators and determined that he had worked at El Taquito off and on since 1989.

"Yes, his name was Enrique Gomez. He was one of those guys who lived on the street and traveled to Mexico and then came back here again. I've known him for years and years, but nobody knows a whole lot about him," Casey said.

He thought Enrique had been in his sixties and not his fifties, as the police had said. He had worked as a janitor at El Taquito and cut the grass. He hadn't been there in more than a year. Everybody liked him. Casey didn't know if anyone knew how to reach his family. Enrique had told Casey his wife had died and he had two adult children. Casey could not say much more about him. He didn't know him well.

I made my way to Southwest Boulevard and asked several Mexicans on the corner if they knew anyone named Enrique. They shook their heads. I returned to Los Alamos and told Augustin what little I'd learned.

"These guys come from Mexico to work," he said. "We don't know where they're from, where they go, where they live. We don't know nothing about them. They die. It's sad."

I left Augustin and called the coroner. After identifying myself as a *Star* reporter, I asked about Enrique. He died, the coroner told me, of a heart attack. Not untypical, he said, for someone so poor.

I got off the phone and wondered whether I had seen Enrique in Los Alamos. I might have said "*Hola*," and he might have responded as the other Mexicans do when I greet them, shy and appreciative of this gesture from someone not part of their community and who doesn't speak Spanish.

One morning I asked Augustin what he thought of all the changes on Summit. He had lost some old customers, he said, but he had picked up a few new ones like myself. As long as business was good, he would be okay, he said. He worried about property values increasing to the point that he could no longer afford his house. He would adapt, work harder. He had a wife and two children to support. He had to worry about himself first.

"I try not to think too much about it," he said, but I could see in his eyes that he thought a great deal about it.

Augustin's immigrant story was no different from those of many of his customers. He was born in Monterrey, Mexico. While he was still a boy, one of his aunts moved to Kansas City. She returned to Monterrey every few months to visit family, and every time she stopped to see his parents, Augustin made her coffee. He was her favorite nephew and she wanted to take him to the States. His father said, "If Augustin goes, we all go." Augustin's aunt hectored the family so much that one day his father said, "Okay, enough. We'll go on a vacation."

His family intended to stay three months. Augustin had just turned seven. When it was time to return to Monterrey, they decided to remain a little longer. And a little longer. And a little longer. Now, decades later, Augustin can look south down Summit and see the small wooden house with a square backyard where he'd grown up. He and his wife and his two US-born children live in it now. Like his father before him, he plays the Mexican national anthem and raises the Mexican flag over his house. He reminds his children where he and their mother came from. Mexico. Never forget, he tells them. Never forget. You are Americans, but do not be embarrassed to be Mexicans too.

Then Enrique died. Then the condominium debate started. Then Adolfo downsized to one rented room. In the fall of 2004, as the community meetings were going on, Augustin raised a Mexican flag on the rooftop of Los Alamos to commemorate Mexico's independence from Spain on September 16, 1810, and to remind newcomers of the Mexicans who still lived on Summit and in the West Side. Many had left; others had died. In too many cases they were people no one remembered. Yet Augustin remembered them. They had worked hard and contributed to defining Summit Street as an immigrant community.

Days after Augustin raised the flag, a man came into Los Alamos and accused Augustin of disloyalty to America. Then a vendor telephoned to warn Augustin that he had heard a caller on local talk radio threatening to remove the flag by force if necessary. "It's bad enough we have illegals," the caller had said. "It's worse when they show their flag like they're proud of it."

"What is the problem?" Augustin asked me. He lived in Kansas City legally. He loved the United States, but he also loved Mexico. He had asked the city if he could put the flag on the roof. The man he spoke to told him he did not need a permit. So why the threats? He had considered taking down the flag, but he decided no, he would let it stand. He would not be intimidated. He asked customers and friends who lived nearby to alert him if they saw anyone take it. He was not trying to do anything against the United States. It was just a flag.

To my knowledge no one attempted to take down the flag, although the threats against Augustin continued for several more weeks and burglars broke into his store twice in the same period. Through it all the flag remained aloft, including the morning a year later when I left for Overland Park, a suburb of Kansas City, to live with my girlfriend.

From time to time as I adjusted to my new life I considered driving to Summit Street to visit the old neighborhood. I wondered if Augustin still owned Los Alamos or if he too had fallen victim to gentrification. Did any Mexican families remain? I'll never know because I never went back. I did not want to see how the changes I had witnessed might have consumed the community. I did not want to see how people like me—spearheading a contemporary version of manifest destiny without caring for what had come before—had caused those changes.

On a windless night, the day before I packed up for Overland Park, I stopped by Los Alamos to say good-bye to Augustin. Mexican day laborers lingered outside talking, killing time, before they made their way home, men I recognized from the neighborhood and I had greeted dozens of times but whose names I did not know. They would get up early the next day and a few minutes before six meander nameless as shadows past what had been Adolfo's house, renovated now by its new owner, past Fausto's home where Enrique had sat in a blue chair singing and sharing tortillas, toward Los Alamos and coffee, the flag limp in the windless morning like something exhausted, drooping against the wooden pole in subdued deflation, not a breath of air to disturb it or the laborers once articulated lingering on the sidewalk, unnoticed now and unwanted.

Flo's House
(2006)

The other week as I followed a dirt path in an industrial area of Kansas City, Missouri, known as the West Bottoms, I found a kitten. Or, I should say, it found me. The trail twisted around trees and over rusted train tracks and past a camp of homeless army veterans. I was a reporter writing a story about federal budget cuts in programs for homeless vets for the *Kansas City Star*. I wanted to ask them what they thought of the reductions.

Just as I was looking for a place to sit, I felt something claw into the back of my right thigh. I jerked around and looked over my shoulder while swatting at my leg. Whatever it was dug in deeper, and I turned faster and faster, cursing, and finally grabbed it but lost my balance and fell. One of the vets stepped over me, bent over and picked up whatever it was that had been squirming in my hand. He looked down at me, the trees behind him towering above us and blocking the sun.

"Cat," he said.

He dropped it, I caught it, and sat up holding a gray kitten.

The vet helped me to my feet. After the interview I searched my pockets for my cell phone and called my partner, Flo.

"I found a kitten," I told her.

"A kitten?" Flo said. "Where?"

I heard her ten-year-old daughter, Molly, shout, "A kitten! Bring it home. Let him bring it home, Mom!"

"Well, it's too late for me to say no now," Flo said, sounding more flustered than upset.

"I want it!" Molly shouted.

"You hear that?" Flo said.

"Flo," I said, pausing to emphasize my point, "the kitten is mine."

My father had felt the same way about a Newfoundland we had when I was growing up. The dog, he said, belonged to him. For years we had owned Great Danes. They always died at an early age, however, from painful stomach disorders common to their breed, and my mother and father grew tired of the heartbreak. When our veterinarian euthanized our third Great Dane just five years after we brought it home, my parents said that's it: no more Danes. A few years passed when we didn't have a dog at all. Then my mother persuaded my father to buy a black standard poodle, a decidedly feminine dog, in his estimation. The poodle accompanied my mother when she shopped, sat with her when she read the newspaper and slept at the foot of her side of the bed. It was her dog, as much as my two older brothers and I were her children. She made our breakfasts, lunches and dinners; bought our clothes; took us to doctor appointments; tucked us in at night. My father would come home from work, read the newspaper and listen to the news. He became increasingly distant as our hormones erupted and we grew into contrary teenagers.

My father never warmed to the poodle. Two years after he gave it to my mother, he bought a second dog: a black Newfoundland, a much heftier breed than a poodle.

"This is my dog," he announced proudly, holding the fat four-month-old, distressed-looking puppy in his arms. However, Gus, the name he gave it, was no more his dog than the poodle was. My father was not home during the day like my mother. He did not housebreak Gus, feed him, walk him, and take him to the veterinarian. Gus followed my mother around the house when my father was home the way the poodle did, because in the end Gus was her dog too.

Twelve years later, I drove with my father to Becker Animal Hospital to have Gus euthanized. His hair was falling out in clumps and he could no longer walk. My father wept as Dr. Becker inserted a needle into Gus's foreleg and pushed the plunger of the syringe. Standing over Gus, my father felt keenly the loss of an animal he knew had never loved him as it had my mother.

I was twenty-two when Gus died and had just graduated from Coe College in Cedar Rapids, Iowa. I was bouncing from state to state, working temp jobs without a clue to a career. My father said I'd turned into a bum. He thought I should work at a bank or in retail and establish myself. Despite his criticism, he never stopped asking me about my travels. He traced my routes on a map. I have never visited that part of the country, he would say, poking at one place and then another. I always wanted to. What was it like? Did you like it? I'll have to go there someday.

I remember sitting on my father's lap as a boy. He would hold my arms, spread his legs and I'd drop through the gap, almost hitting the floor before he pulled me back up, and I would laugh, eager for more. I remember walking beside him, trying to keep up with his long stride. We would play catch together in the backyard. I felt the hard smack of the ball when he hurled it into my hands. I remember spilling a glass of milk at the dinner table. I was about five or six. My father threatened to beat me with his shoe. I can still see the glass slipping from my grasp, the milk gushing out in slow motion as my father's face blossomed with fury.

I inherited his temper. When I was nine years old, my childhood friend Tom and his parents were late picking me up for a Chicago Cubs game. I thought we'd miss the first inning. I stomped my feet and kicked the breakfast nook table.

"Where are they?" I snapped.

"You're acting just like your father," my mother scolded.

Her words stopped me cold. I sat down and took deep breaths, letting each one out slowly, until I calmed down. I would not be my father.

Flo had been divorced for five years when we met in 2002. She had read a story of mine in the *Star* about a puppy I had rescued from a dog fight in Kabul that year. In an email she praised me for saving the dog. She also said she liked a photo of me that accompanied the story and suggested we get together. Intrigued by how direct she was, and flattered, I agreed.

We met at Kaldis, a coffee shop in Kansas City's Country Club Plaza, on a Saturday in mid-March. Flo wore a snug white blouse and blue jeans, and I liked how her clothes hugged her body and the way her blond hair fell down her back. We soon realized we had several things in common. Flo was a social worker in a high school in Shawnee, Kansas, a suburb of Kansas City. I told her about my work with the homeless in San Francisco. She had lived in Columbia, Missouri. I had too when I was traipsing across the country in my twenties. We were both vegetarians. At the time, I still lived on Summit Street. Flo owned a two-story home in Overland Park, Kansas, where she lived with her two teenage sons, Barry and Danny, and Molly. Barry was about to graduate from high school.

Flo and I spent two hours together in the Plaza. I asked her out for dinner a few days later. We dated for more than a year before I moved in. Few things in Flo's house belonged to me. If I put something away where it hadn't been before she would call me on it. Not because it didn't make sense but because I was breaking an established order. Molly treated me like the younger sibling she never had, a cross between friendship and total disregard. Barry and Danny were deep into their teenage worlds and had little use for me.

Although Flo and I referred to her house as "our house," I wasn't fooling myself. The house remained very much hers. In stressful moments she talked as if she still lived alone. She complained, "My grass needs to be cut," or "My bedroom is a mess," or "My kitchen is too small." At these times, I was reminded about who the house belonged to, and I felt like a tenant who was sleeping with the landlady. I lived inside Flo's house but outside it too, an observer one step removed from the activity around me. Our life together took on the feel of another reporting assignment that would end.

Weekdays Flo and I would wake up about six and get ready for work. Molly would catch a bus to school about seven-thirty. At night Flo would cook dinner. Afterward she would go over Molly's homework and then we would read or watch television together. In no time at all, it seemed, it was time for bed.

On weekends I still got up early. I made coffee and waited for her to come downstairs. Then we'd eat breakfast, clean the house, and take Molly to a movie. Before I knew it, we were having dinner and then kissing good night, long kisses that sometimes put the night on hold before it raced ahead again toward dawn. Hours later I rose to the surface from a deep sleep, awaking to another day in Flo's house.

Shortly after I moved in, we discussed buying a house that would be truly "ours," but neither of us had the money and we didn't want to go into debt. After some consideration, we arrived at an alternative plan. We decided to replace the tiled floors in the kitchen, living room, and front hall of Flo's house with hardwood. Altering the interior, we thought, would make the house as much mine as hers.

The morning I'd found the kitten, the house was in upheaval. Carpenters had been in the previous day and had begun work on the floors. Piles of shorn tile took up corners. Living room rugs had been heaped on top of chairs. End tables appeared to have been tossed into any out-of-the-way place.

"Look what they've done to my house," Flo said, greeting me at the door.

Kitten in tow, I had parked on the street outside Flo's house. She kept her car in the garage. She got home from work before I did and felt that entitled her to the space. I didn't argue; it made sense, I supposed. What I did know was that I left my car on the street. It meant that I locked the doors every night. It meant that my car was exposed. It meant that I hoped some kid didn't vandalize it. Sometimes such little patterns of our life together combusted and I wanted to explode and leave Flo. Instead, I'd walk around the block and recall when we'd gotten together at Kaldis Coffee. Her blond hair, the sparkle in her eyes. The way she said good-bye with a cock of her head and a coquettish twist of her hips. Remembering these moments, I felt the rush of warm feelings I'd had when we first met. I was sure I'd miss Flo, even those moments when she upset me, because those moments were part of her companionship, part of what filled me and made me feel not alone.

Resolving to control my temper but still feeling annoyed, I'd return to the house and say nothing. My father would have stormed back inside and let rip a hurricane of fury. I instead engaged in silence, retreating to the study and turning on the computer to cut myself off from Flo, from Molly, from everyone, allowing the flame of my anger to smolder and sputter out.

"You okay?," Flo asked.

"I'm fine," I told her.

I carried the kitten inside, and Molly met me at the door and lifted it from my arms.

"Can I keep her in my room?" she asked Flo.

"I don't see why not."

"Wait," I said. "We don't even know if it's litter-trained. We'll put it in our bathroom tonight and see how it does."

"We'll put it in the bathroom now and if it's okay in a couple of hours, I don't see why she can't have it in her room," Flo answered.

She looked at me with a what-do-you-want-me-to-do expression. I gave her my don't-give-your-daughter-everything-she-wants look.

What? Flo said with her eyes. What are you saying?

"Nothing," I said. "Nothing."

"This is a big step," Flo said when I decided to move in with her.

"Are you sure?"

"Of course."

Until then we'd had a routine: I'd spend several nights a week with her and then return to my apartment. Sofa, chair, futon bed, television, bare walls. I met friends after work at bars, or, I drove home and watched TV. A day or two later I'd stay with Flo again. Something was missing. I felt alive only when I traveled abroad as a reporter, invigorated by the impermanence and uncertainties of the journey. I had nothing to look forward to in Kansas City until I met Flo. I thought moving in with her would be the start of our lives together. I thought I'd feel settled. I thought I'd be content.

"Of course," I said again. "I have to do something."

"*We* have to," she corrected.

That night I thought of my parents. My father was thirty-two and my mother twenty-nine when they married, old by the standards of their World War II generation. They had to do something. I don't think, however, that they were desperate.

A black-and-white photo of my parents shows them sitting in a restaurant at a table filled with other people. Baskets of flowers hang above their heads. My mother wears a light-colored dress, my father a suit and tie. They're smiling at each other. Their eyes dance with mischief. I imagine them reaching beneath the table toward each other in this room crowded with other couples oblivious of their desire.

I understood just how much my parents loved each other not long ago when my mother tripped while walking into the kitchen from the living room and fell against a wall. She slid to the floor bleeding from her forehead.

My father helped her back up and then grabbed her coat. He insisted on taking her to the emergency room no matter her objections. I was home visiting. I drove and he directed me although I knew the way. I kept quiet and let him take charge in the only way he could, since his failing eyesight prevented him from driving.

Seated on a gurney waiting to be examined, my mother muttered about how she hated hospitals. My father, she said, was making a fuss over nothing. He laughed. He patted her knee and she reached over and covered his hand with hers. She didn't stop complaining until the doctors released her. My father kept smiling and laughing and holding her hand. Her fingers entwined with his and he put his other hand over hers and they looked at each other as if I weren't there.

I blushed. I could not recall ever having seen them kiss, let alone hold hands.

When I moved in with Flo, I stored my sofa, chair, and futon in her basement and covered them with a plastic sheet. A room upstairs had been cleared for me to use as a study. I had suggested putting my futon there to use it as a couch, but Flo said it didn't go with the pink carpet. The study was just inside the front door and was the first room a visitor would see on entering the house. She wanted me to get new furniture. I bought two wicker chairs with red cushions. She liked the chairs at first, but when I brought them home she thought they were uncomfortable, and she hated the southwestern pattern on the cushions.

"You didn't want the futon and now you don't like the chairs," I said.

We ignored each other the rest of the day. The following afternoon I dropped by her work and brought her roses. She cried. We had lunch and stitched our life back together.

We called the kitten Zoey. Molly decided on the name. When she went to bed, Molly took it into her room. Flo and I would stay up and watch television. Then Flo went to bed. If I wasn't tired, I'd go into the kitchen and pour a glass of red wine. Then I'd open a can of cat food and wait. In seconds, Zoey ran downstairs. I took satisfaction in watching her eat. When she finished, I walked into the living room and considered the disaster the carpenters had made.

Moving through the clutter, I began to organize things. I pushed the sofa against the wall and placed the end tables on either side of it. I laid the rugs over the exposed subfloor and plugged in a lamp and set up some chairs. It didn't look much better, but now it was *my* mess.

Then I carried Zoey downstairs to the basement and sat on my futon. The plastic sheet crinkled under me. It had the same smell as a new car.

My father used to tell me stories about his first job as a salesman with a Baltimore canning company before he went to work for his father. He'd drive to Omaha, Denver, Santa Fe. Rolling past farm fields and silent houses. No radio. Cocooned in his car, floating in the silence of early morning. He enjoyed talking about it and drifted off for seconds with his eyes closed before he turned to me, opened his eyes, and waited for the present to reassert itself.

I continued feeding Zoey at night, and she stopped sleeping with Molly. Now she follows me around until I'm ready for bed. Although she wants to sleep with me, her loud purr keeps Flo awake. I lock Zoey out of the room but some nights she scratches at the door, waking us both.

"We need to put Zoey in the basement at night," Flo told me one night before dinner.

We faced each other in the kitchen. I poured two glasses of wine.

"If you ignore her, she'll stop," I said.

"I can't keep taking sleeping pills every night."

"She won't understand what you're doing if you lock her in the basement."

"Listen to you. She's a cat."

"Well, it's your house, isn't it? Do what you want."

"I don't even know what you mean by that."

I stepped back into a corner, gripping my wineglass. I stared at the floor and fought back my temper. Flo crossed her arms and looked away. I waited, feeling we were at a defining moment in our relationship, that when we spoke again we would either cobble together an acceptable agreement or we would not, and that would be it. Or the start of being it.

Flo turned away from me and began emptying the dishwasher. A dessert plate slipped from her hand. I watched it fall, watched it shatter near my feet.

"I'm sorry," Flo said, her voice breaking.

I nudged pieces of glass with my shoe. I now felt calm, almost serene. The noise of the broken plate had dispersed my anger into the silence that followed. I felt a calm so total I didn't need to say one word. I just stood there and reset, holding my wineglass and listening to Flo cry.

The two young men installing the floor, Craig and Dennis, looked about the same age I was when I worked on a construction crew one summer during college in Cedar Rapids. We were building a hotel. The morning they started work I helped them unload boxes of nails and glue from their truck. They appeared uncomfortable with my assistance but not quite sure what to do about it. I told them stories about my summer in Cedar Rapids: the incompetence of the supervisor, the sweltering heat, the twelve-to-fifteen-hour days. That day I kept pace with Craig and Dennis until we finished working. I invited them into the kitchen and made coffee and offered them doughnuts. I told more stories. They stopped calling me Mr. Garcia. They said if I wanted to, I could work with them the next day.

When I look back on that college summer, I remember a wheelbarrow filled with cement and the weight of its wooden handles in my hands as I lift it, and I feel the muscles in my arms tense when I push forward, and just when it seems the wheelbarrow will not budge it begins to roll, carried by the weight of the cement, and I shove it up a wobbly board, nothing below me but a trench of gravel and mud, and onto the second floor of the hotel and tip it, dumping the cement into a trough, and then let go of the handles and the wheelbarrow stands for seconds and then falls sideways and I rest my hands on my hips and catch my breath free of its weight, sweating, my arms inflated from the strain, and I look out at Cedar Rapids and the flat roofs and the splashes of green between houses and the long roads like tentacles that ensnare neighborhoods as well as lead out of them, and I see my father on one of those roads and think that if my pounding heart does not slow down I will walk on air, by God, walk on air right over everything and follow him out of town.

One morning Craig told me we had a problem. He had removed the toilet to lay the floor in the second-floor bathroom and found that the mount for the toilet had rotted.

"You need a plumber to take care of this," he said.

"I need my bathroom," Flo said.

"I don't do plumbing."

"But . . ." I began.

"Dude," Craig said. "I don't do this kind of work."

He walked downstairs. Shadows dappled his body and it appeared for an instant that he was descending into water. He stopped at a plate of doughnuts and popped the last one in his mouth. The camaraderie was over. He didn't care about my summer in Cedar Rapids. I had worked beside him and Dennis, and they were the ones getting paid. He was probably laughing at me.

"Where're you going?" I said.

"Truck."

He opened the door and Zoey darted outside.

"Oh, Christ," I said.

Zoey dashed across the yard to some trees and I ran after her. She took off again, bounding farther away. I kept running. Flo shouted after me. I ran faster and faster, disconnected from a lonely desire to hold her one last time, until I heard nothing but my feet cutting through the damp grass, and I passed trees and more trees and continued running toward what I didn't know, the sound of my father calling me back yet urging me on.

A Simple Explanation

(2005–2008)

I was asleep the night Chris died. The year was 2005. According to news reports, Chris had just returned home from college a week before Christmas and was driving at night with his sister. They had been very close. She was the first person other than his parents he wanted to see. It was also reported that he enjoyed driving fast and was a NASCAR fan. The accident happened around midnight, a block from his house in Overland Park, Kansas, not far from where I lived on 115th Terrace. I thought his death tragic but didn't think much more about it until the following year, when my brother Butch died just as unexpectedly.

What I had heard about Chris reminded me of Butch. Like Chris, Butch enjoyed driving fast. As a teenager he'd fancied himself a race car driver. His obsession followed an earlier infatuation with scuba diving. In high school he bought a mask and flippers and a deep-sea watch and subscribed to diving magazines. Yet he never took lessons, although our parents offered to pay for them.

When I was eleven and Butch was eighteen, our family vacationed in Bermuda. We stayed at a hotel that offered scuba lessons. I asked Butch to sign up with me. We would learn in a pool and then later in the afternoon dive in the ocean. He sat on the edge of his bed and stared at the floor, cornered by my excitement and the opportunity. His face paled.

"I'm not feeling good, Moose," he said.

I took the lessons alone. My mother wanted Butch to see the hotel doctor, but my father insisted he was fine.

"He's afraid," my father concluded, disgusted. "Not sick."

My mother did not respond. She knew better. My father was not someone who accepted inhibition, especially not from his eldest son and namesake, Charles Jr. As a consequence, my mother held herself accountable for whatever fears prevented Butch from pursuing his interests. When he started school, he had trouble reading and repeated first grade. My mother believed his self-confidence was damaged from that moment on. My father dismissed the idea with an impatient mutter of "Nonsense." Still, she persisted in her belief that she was responsible for my brother's lack of confidence. She was convinced that if she had only insisted that he go on to the second grade with the rest of his class his life might have been different.

When we returned home from Bermuda, Butch shelved his mask and flippers in his bedroom closet, canceled his subscriptions to scuba magazines, and became fixated on race cars. He covered the walls of his bedroom with posters of GT-R and F1 cars. Stacks of *Road & Track* magazines filled the corners of his room. He started driving with his arms locked at the elbows like the great Mario Andretti and took curves at high speed. He could imagine whatever he wanted when he was behind the wheel of our father's Mustang, out of sight of his scorn and a little brother too young to drive.

Chris skidded across a median strip on Antioch Road and into oncoming traffic when he lost control of his car. Miraculously, he struck only one other car. Just as amazing, its driver, while shaken, was uninjured. Chris's car overturned onto a sidewalk where it came to a rest upside down, wheels spinning. His sister survived.

Chris's family lived not far from me. I didn't know them. A neighbor pointed out their house, a one-story home of brown stone and red bricks with a small lawn and sloping driveway. I saw no one, only an array of cars in the driveway. Relatives. Mourners. Unaware of the accident, a passerby might have assumed the family had company for the holidays. The same passerby would likely have thought the same thing had they seen the people filing into our house when Butch died three days after Christmas in 2006.

I wanted to feel bad about Chris, but I felt no more than a kind of intellectual regret, what I always feel when I learn about the death of someone I don't know who has died needlessly. Like a tornado picking off one house while leaving others untouched, his dying seemed too random, too purposeless, thrust upon the neighborhood by circumstances over which we had no control, leaving those of us who hadn't known Chris wondering what to think, what to say.

On the other hand, I haven't come to terms with Butch's death, someone I obviously knew quite well. It hovers around me, lurking silently, springing out of nowhere when I least expect to be reminded of him. And now, recalling Chris, so much like my brother in at least one respect, I'm missing Butch once more.

A week before he died, Butch called to tell me he had married Carol, his live-in girlfriend, in a brief ceremony before a Chicago judge. He did so, he said, "for the health care." He was unemployed, and she was working and had benefits. I thought he was just posturing but he persisted, and I couldn't help but notice the concern in his voice, even fear.

"I don't know what's happening," he said. "I'm eating right, eating my vegetables, I'm not drinking, but I keep putting on weight. I need to see a doctor."

Three years of sitting around unemployed, eating fast food, knocking off soda after soda and indulging in too much booze had taken its toll. He was obese. Now, I thought, he's become so huge, so uncomfortable, that he wants to do something about it. Finally.

"That's good," I said about the doctor. "See what he says."

Butch had a checkup the day after Christmas. He told my parents the doctor had prescribed a diuretic to reduce fluid buildup. Other than that, Butch said, he was in good health. Blood pressure normal.

Lungs clear. Lab tests negative. My father said he didn't believe him. Two days later, an ambulance rushed Butch to a hospital.

The day after Butch died, I drove nine hours from Overland Park to my parents' home in Winnetka. I arrived at night and let myself in through the garage and entered the kitchen. No lights. The hall consumed me. I put out my hands, groping for a light switch, and called out to my mother and father.

"Who's there?" they both said from the living room, sounding confused and fearful, as if I were another shock of bad news.

"It's all right," I said. "It's me, just me."

My mother shuffled into the kitchen, her damp, red-rimmed eyes small pools of grief. She hugged me and then withdrew without a word to the couch in the living room. She stared without seeing out the terrace window. My father asked about my drive.

"It was fine."

"It's good to see you. I'm sorry it had to be like this."

He turned off the hall light. Even in grief, he would not waste electricity. In the sudden blackness, I heard my father searching for answers.

"It happened so fast," he said. "It doesn't make sense. I spoke to him the day before."

My eyes slowly adjusted to the dark. I walked into the living room and sat beside my parents without speaking, Butch making his presence felt by his absence.

Friends of Chris held an evening prayer vigil near where his car had overturned. They stuck a small artificial Christmas tree in the ground and lit candles around it, and placed a small white cross surrounded by plastic-wrapped roses against a streetlight on the median strip. *Chris, we'll always remember that dreadful night,* someone wrote. The cross shone at night beneath the light, the roses full and open. A few days later snow fell in heavy white clumps and the cross collapsed from the weight. When the weather warmed, the cross lay in mud streaked with slush. The roses had curled but had maintained their color.

When I was sixteen, I myself came close to ending up like Chris when I nearly crashed into a tree head-on during Christmas break. It was my junior year in high school, and I was driving a car that belonged to the parents of my friend Tom. At sixteen we knew only the thrill of the present and the need to show off, convinced that the faster we drove the more power we had, the cooler we were. I turned onto Woodley Road and accelerated to sixty miles an hour. I turned left at a fork in the snow-covered road, slipping into a skid. I spun the wheel left and then right, getting increasingly frantic. Tom screamed *Brake! Brake!* I slammed on the brakes and veered off the road into some woods. Tree branches raked the side of the car and dead leaves and clumps of snow struck the windshield. I hurtled forward against the steering wheel and gasped. Tom banged his forehead against the dashboard. We didn't say anything. Snow-covered bushes around us sucked in all sound except for our rapid breathing. We were inches from an oak tree.

Tom told me to get out, and we switched places. He backed the car onto the street and we saw the deep gouges the tires had made where I'd spun off the road. We drove to my house. The gray grit on the car was slashed with crooked lines. We couldn't tell how badly, if at all, the car had been scratched.

I told my parents we wanted to surprise Tom's mother by washing her car. I filled a bucket with steaming hot water and grabbed two fat sponges from our garage. My father followed me outside without putting on his coat. He said the water would freeze on the car. Tom and I wiped it down anyway, washing away the dirt. Our wet hands stung from the cold and turned pink. My father shook his head, watching the water bead into ice.

"You're not making any sense," he said.

As the grime sluiced off, we saw there were only a few minor scratches. Tom's parents would never notice. We slapped each other on the back, invincible again.

"Get inside!" my mother shouted at my father. "You'll catch your death of cold."

He waved her away. Crossing his arms against the wind he frowned, trying to comprehend our logic.

"You'll catch pneumonia!" my mother shouted.

It took years of ignoring her, but eventually my mother was proved right. In 2004, Butch and Michael called me in Overland Park to say that our eighty-nine-year-old father had been hospitalized with pneumonia. He had gone out into the cold without a coat once too often. I had known something was wrong; when I called home, my father coughed and cleared his throat every two or three words. My mother pleaded with him to see a doctor. He refused. Then one night, unable to talk, his chest aching with every breath, and clutching his left side, he relented and my mother drove him to Highland Park Hospital. He allowed himself to be admitted without complaint.

He stayed in the hospital for about two weeks. I remained in Overland Park but spoke to him daily by phone. He sounded exhausted, his voice hoarse. He struggled for breath between words but he insisted he was fine.

"Call your mother," he said. "Check on her for me."

My mother spent her days with him in his hospital room and her evenings at home alone. Our house was a rambling two-story structure with five bedrooms. My mother had hoped to have six children, but she married late and had only three. Without my father there, it must have seemed like wandering through a museum, with darkness enveloping rooms we never used, the photos of my two brothers and me ghostly on the walls, the grandfather clock in the front hall ticking off the seconds. My mother would sit in the living room on the side of the sofa where my father usually sat. The light from the lamp on the end table reflected off a growing stack of magazines she intended to read but never did.

I called her every night. When she didn't pick up I'd leave a message and she would call back almost immediately and apologize.

"I was asleep," she'd say in a weary voice, sounding adrift in the vacant house. "I expected your father to get it. Then I remembered he wasn't here."

My father recovered, thinner for the effort, and bad-tempered.

"He's nervous," my mother would say. "He won't sit still."

When I asked my father how he felt, I sensed him searching for words, trying to articulate what he thought of being hospitalized at eighty-nine and surviving when he had already exceeded the average life expectancy of most men by fifteen years.

"I'm glad to be eating home cooking," he said finally, and forced a laugh before he passed the receiver to my mother.

I asked Butch what he thought. "Pop looks great," he told me. "You'd never know how sick he was."

He never divulged that he had not visited our father in the hospital.

Butch was fifty-four then. After high school he attended Hanover College in Indiana. After he graduated, Northrop Grumman, a defense contractor, hired him as an accountant. He lived at home until he was thirty-five. When he moved out, he bought a house and met Carol. In 2002 Northrop laid him off after more than thirty years. He found another job, at Northwestern University, where Carol worked, but a year later he was laid off again. He gave up. He stayed home. He drank. He ate. He lived off his savings and Carol's income.

Sometimes when we got together, Butch would slip back into race-car-driving mode. Elbows locked, foot heavy on the pedal. He was quiet during those moments, perhaps even desperate, the wind coming through the windows and blowing his hair, his sunglasses concealing whatever he might have been thinking.

He gained weight until he appeared inflated. He sounded out of breath. My mother worried about him much as she'd hounded my father to wear a jacket in the cold. She urged me to talk to Butch but I didn't know what to say, discomfited just by looking at him. Even his face had grown puffy.

"He's a grown man," I said, sounding like my father. "He'll do what he wants. Nothing I can do about it."

On Thursday morning, December 28, 2006, Butch woke up struggling to breathe. Carol helped him out of bed. Paramedics rushed him to a hospital. He stopped breathing in the ambulance, dead of congestive heart failure.

The what-ifs come at night.

What if Butch had taken better care of himself?

What if he had seen the doctor earlier?

What if the doctor had admitted him?

What if I had talked to him about his weight?

What if I had said I love you, Butch, don't kill yourself?

His obituary listed his age, occupation, and surviving family members, summarizing his life in a small, two-hundred-word square of copy surrounded by other names in equally small squares. No photograph. What he never achieved in life was not recorded in print. He, his story, was edited down to its essence. Two hundred words, no more. Gone. Just like that.

Michael called me the day Butch died, and then I heard from Carol. Her voice was measured but worn. I was too shocked to ask questions. She told me that when she woke up that morning, Butch sat beside her in bed clutching his chest. He looked scared, confused. Carol called 911. Butch became frantic.

"Did you call?" he asked her again and again, struggling to breathe. "What's taking them so long?" Carol stared out the bedroom window, phone in hand, as if that would make the paramedics arrive faster.

The approaching scream of an ambulance must have reassured them both. It was only seven o'clock. Clear blue skies, light coming through the curtains, snow on the front lawn, their neighbors leaving for work.

The medics examined Butch and thought he might be having an asthma attack. They gave him oxygen, then helped him onto a gurney. He appeared to relax. The medics would figure it out. They would find an answer. A simple explanation. He might have to stay in the hospital overnight, nothing more.

"Don't let the cat out," he told Carol.

Inside the ambulance, Butch closed his eyes.

"Don't let the cat out," he said again.

Carol's voice quivered, overcome by emotion before sinking again into an exhausted monotone.

"When will you get here?"

"As soon as I can," I told her.

I got off the phone. My heart pounded. My hands shook. I thought, *I've got to call work. I must cancel my appointments. I must call an airline for a flight home.* I repeated in a half whisper, "My brother died, my brother died, my brother died," until I knew I could say it without breaking down. Then I called my editor at the *Star*.

"I'm sorry," he said.

"So am I."

Next, I canceled a dentist appointment, then called United Airlines. I explained what had happened and that I needed a flight to Chicago from Kansas City immediately. The man on the line demanded proof of Butch's death.

"What hospital was he seen at?"

I didn't know.

"What funeral home was he at?"

I didn't know.

"What time did he die?"

"Today, this morning. I don't know exactly."

The man told me I couldn't get a bereavement flight without answering these questions. I insisted I just wanted a flight, not a special rate. He hung up. I slammed the receiver against the kitchen table until it slid out of my hand, and I covered my face and wept.

Today is the second anniversary of Butch's death. A clear morning, absent of clouds. No snow. Unseasonably warm, with temperatures somewhere in the mid-forties. The cool air reminds me more of fall than winter. Squirrels romp across bare lawns and Christmas lights frame doors and garages. I did not remember what day it was until this evening, when I called a friend to wish her happy birthday. As her phone rang it hit me: Butch died today. I hung up before she answered, stunned that I had forgotten.

A blind woman I know told me that with each passing day it gets harder and harder for her to remember what it was like to see. I wonder if something similar is happening with my memories of Butch. My life has changed these past two years while his has ceased. Since he died, I've reported from Afghanistan, Pakistan, and Chad. I broke up with my girlfriend and moved back to Kansas City from Overland Park. The economy tanked. I worried about my job. I turned fifty, then fifty-one. It seems long ago that I was forty-nine and looking at my brother's coffin. I still recall how we'd get together to wash his car or watch the Chicago Bears and share some beers. I hear his booming laugh. Memories increasingly distant, never to be repeated.

Some things haven't changed. I telephone my parents every Sunday, as I did when Butch was alive. We compare the weather in Chicago and Kansas City, complain about it being too hot or too cold. After a brief pause we struggle for other things to talk about, but they don't have much to say. Their advanced age confines them more and more to the house and limits their participation in my world of movies and restaurants, politics and gossip, travel abroad and in the States.

"So, what have you been doing?" they ask me.

I tell them, launching into a kind of one-man act for which they are the audience, because I'm the one doing the doing, not them.

Sometimes I find myself subtracting the year of my parents' births from the current year, grateful they have lived long lives but aware that they will not live forever. I know eventually I'll get a call about one of them, as I did about Butch.

I had just deposited a check and was still in the bank parking lot when Michael reached me on my cell phone.

"I have terrible news," he said.

"Pop again?"

"No."

"Mom?"

"No, Butch. He died."

I didn't say anything. My car seemed to contract around me until it felt horribly claustrophobic. I unrolled my window for air. People strolled through the parking lot but I didn't hear them. Michael began crying. I sat and listened to him for a long time, speechless.

On a whim this morning, I drove with my dogs to Overland Park and stopped at the memorial for Chris. The worn cross still stood slanted in the ground. I placed it against the lamppost and wiped it clean. Three years. I'm surprised how it has endured. I wonder if it will be here next year. I doubt it. If there's such a thing as life after death, I believe, it's in the memories we have and the ways people no longer here continue to influence us and live on in our own behavior. I won't forget Butch. Chris either. Cross or no cross.

My dogs tugged at their leashes. I waited for traffic to pass, then ran with them across the street to the sidewalk. We started walking, and the day resumed with us, the sun advancing across the sky, everything moving forward, only differently, no one the same.

The Castle

(2007)

The owner of the Castle issued an ultimatum yesterday:

Back off or suffer the consequences. At least, that's my father's interpretation of what he said. My father knows only that the owner sent a letter to the Woodley Road Neighborhood Association after his power lines were cut the other week, and he was none too pleasant in what he wrote. He's a rich, high-powered Chicago attorney, which leads my father to all sorts of nervous speculation about what he might do.

"I'm told he's under the impression it was people from around here who cut his power lines," my father says. "He accused association members themselves of doing it. He thinks they were also the ones who tore up his sod and marked his driveway with graffiti two weeks ago."

I drove here from Kansas City to spend the weekend with my parents at my brother Michael's request. He called me this afternoon to say he'd be here later tonight but not in time for dinner. I told my parents, and my mother said he could have dessert with us. What they don't know is that Michael wants to talk to them about moving, about leaving the house where they've lived since 1957 for an assisted-living home.

I go into the kitchen and ask my mother for some plates. My father gets napkins from a cupboard, and together we set the table. My mother stays in the kitchen heating a large frozen pizza.

"The association tried to stop him in court from building the Castle and later objected when he added the wall around it," my father continues. "All the members deny any involvement in the vandalism. I don't know what to believe. If it doesn't stop, he'll do something. I don't blame him; I'd do something too. I don't belong to the association but I bet he'll take it out on the whole neighborhood, whether you're a member or not. He thinks we're all against him. I was opposed to him building the Castle but I'm not against him."

My father looks at me. I hand him the plates. He sets them on the table.

"He has a right to live here, is what I mean," my father says. "I just wish he hadn't built that thing."

Replete with minarets, balconies, archways, and walkways, the four-story square stone mansion my parents have nicknamed the Castle sprawls on three acres of land. Its owner bought the property from the Yarnald family. I only vaguely remember the Yarnalds, yet I can still see their white two-story house and the three yapping miniature schnauzers they walked every day no matter the weather. Hedges of evergreen shrubs and towering elms concealed their house from the road, and I would often hear their dogs barking furiously, following me from behind the hedges as I walked past their property to school.

The street my parents live on was named Woodley Road by its developer. When I was a child, elms concealed houses from one another and absorbed the noise from Hill Street and Illinois Road and Skokie Highway 41 and other busy roadways outside the neighborhood. Their heavy branches provided shade in the summer and helped block frigid winds blowing off Lake Michigan in the winter.

The owner of the Castle bought the Yarnald property two years ago and tore down the house to erect his estate. It did not go well at first. The new foundation cracked. Once that issue was resolved, construction resumed and the monolithic size of his ambition soon became apparent. Neighbors recognized that once completed, the Castle would obscure the view from their own expansive homes.

Petitions were distributed and signed, and the neighborhood association took the Castle's owner to court in the hope of scaling down the size of his mansion, but the case was thrown out, my father says. He doesn't know the details but suspects that money, personal connections, and property rights trumped zoning laws and the neighborhood's objections.

Last year the Castle's owner built a ten-foot brick wall around his property and in the process cut down fifteen elms. The neighbors took him to court again. Something about infringement, property lines, and building too close to the road. That case was also thrown out.

"People asked us to get involved, so I said, 'Sure, I'll sign your petition, but that's as far as I'll go,'" my father says. "I didn't want any trouble. This guy knows what he's doing. He's a lawyer, after all. He's got it all laid out. He knows people who greased the wheels for him, I'm sure. I wish I hadn't signed that petition. I'd rather he not get hold of my name."

"So now he thinks the neighbors are out to get him by vandalizing his property because they failed in court?" I say.

"He's not popular, for sure," my father says.

"I don't think much of anyone who kills fifteen trees," my mother observes.

She tells me the pizza is ready, and I take it out of the oven and slide it onto a cutting board. I look for a knife to slice it.

"It's not just the trees," my father says, pulling out a chair for my mother at the table. "I hate seeing old homes torn down."

"It's like losing a member of the family," my mother says.

My father is ninety-two, my mother ninety. They read the *Chicago Tribune*, the *Wall Street Journal*, and the *New York Times*, and prefer listening to the radio to watching TV. On occasion they still go out to a restaurant, but not often. I want to believe they're just fine, but I can't help noticing that they no longer maintain the house and to some degree themselves.

My mother has curvature of the spine and is blind in one eye. Arthritis has curled her fingers into hooks. She does little more than sit in one place for most of the day and stare into space when she's not reading. My father has a bad heart. He continues to drive and does the grocery shopping, but the dents on the front and rear of his car testify that he shouldn't get behind the wheel.

The house itself has become something of a wreck. I don't know when my parents last cleaned the living room carpet. They fail to notice that its stink sucks the oxygen from the room. The chipped and cracked wooden floor needs to be waxed if not replaced, and moths have harvested the draperies. Layers of dust mantle the furniture. In the kitchen, encrusted pots and pans fill a cabinet beneath the oven. The grimy gas stove has ensnared ants in pockets of goop, and only one burner works. My mother washes some of their clothes by hand in the kitchen sink because it's become increasingly difficult for her to walk downstairs into the basement to use the washing machine. Socks, T-shirts, and underwear drip dry in their bathroom. I've suggested that they hire a maid. They tell me they don't need anyone helping them.

At one time they did consider moving into an apartment, but never followed through. I don't think they looked very hard. Sentiment keeps them on Woodley Road. They can account for each year they've lived in the house by the big and little moments they experienced in it: the births of my older brothers and me, the death of JFK, the Chicago ice storm of 1968 during which my brother and I skated on the lawn, the raccoon trapped in the basement in 1973 and the mess it made, Nixon's resignation, the time Michael broke his arm, and so on. These are the mile markers of my parents' life together, the passage of years in which they saw themselves age and the house along with them. Their stooped backs, its warped walls. Their gray hair, its chipped paint. Their lined faces, its worn look. The house holds their history. Remaining in it must be akin to holding on to one of the few friends they have left.

My mother feels sure the house will be torn down like the Yarnalds' someday. In her mind a far more imposing, perhaps even more sinister monstrosity than the Castle will rise from the rubble of our demolished home. Something so huge that its engulfing presence will obliterate any memory of my father and her and the family they raised.

Michael cares little about the fate of the house. He has a wife and daughter, owns his home in Barrington, Illinois, and has no emotional attachment to Woodley Road. I, on the other hand, have rented apartments my entire adult life and have always understood that nothing in them belonged to me except my furniture, clothes, kitchen utensils, and the few pictures I've hung on the walls.

As a reporter, I'm often on the road for weeks, sometimes longer. It doesn't make sense for me to own a house I'd rarely occupy. Apartment living and month-to-month rentals allow me the flexibility to pack up and leave when I'm given an extended assignment. I enjoy traveling and immersing myself in cultures different from my own, the mental chess game of reporting from a foreign place. Still, I can appreciate what I'm missing: stability and a home and a family of my own. That's why I enjoy the times when I visit my parents and sleep in my old bed, surrounded by the detritus of boxed childhood toys and curling Jethro Tull and Santana posters and the memories and sense of place they hold.

Past is past, Michael likes to say. He's a banker, a numbers guy, while I'm the wandering scribe. He could no more live the way I do than I could sit down with a calculator and think what a fine way this is to spend a day. We're not close, but I don't mean to suggest that we dislike each other. We're like two regulars of a bar or coffee shop. We exchange pleasantries and then go our separate ways.

We get together only when a task or problem arises that requires collaboration.

Such as now.

Michael doesn't think it makes sense for our parents to pay property taxes on a house much too big for just the two of them. He wants them to live in Meadowlark, an assisted-living complex near him. The dining hall, he told me, serves three meals a day, and our parents would be required to eat there several times a week to ensure that they don't "isolate." Their "socialization skills" would increase through field trips and other group activities. They would stay active by developing "community engagement plans." For the next four months, Meadowlark is having a move-in special. Michael wants our parents to take advantage of it and is coming over tonight to speak with them about selling the house.

He called me in Kansas City last week. "Would you come up and be there when I talk to them?" he asked me. "If they see we both think it's a good thing for them to do, I think they'll consider it."

They might consider it but they won't like the idea, we both know. No matter how Michael frames it, he'll be asking them to leave the home they have lived in for decades for a new place in a different town. I could see it from their vantage point.

When I was ten minutes from my parents' house, I stopped at Meir's Tavern to fortify myself with a quick beer. The tavern was a favorite stomping ground for my friend Tom and me when we were in college. It dates back to the 1920s and has changed little since then. Deep holes gouged the gravel parking lot. Small square tables with plastic red-checkered tablecloths crowded the wooden floor beneath blinking beer signs. Long ago, cigarette and cigar smoke, now prohibited by law, glazed a mural on the wall a light brown. Ceiling fans creaked and dispersed the aroma of grilled cheeseburgers.

I took a seat at the bar. The bartender gave me a beer and resumed talking to a guy next to me about playing in a rock band.

He had some CDs and set them on the bar for anyone interested. I picked one up.

"CDs are almost too much of a good thing," the bartender said. "Now everybody is recording. Doesn't matter how bad they are. Used to be you had to really earn your chops before you cut a record. Now quality acts are competing against thousands of amateurs. Breaking out is even harder today than before."

His CD had a red cover with head shots of the band members etched in black. I assumed that the bartender lived not too far from Meir's. I imagined him at night sitting on his couch and looking out the window at passing traffic. He strums tunes he hears in his head, searching for a song. He's visible to those drivers who look his way, and then, blip, he's gone.

I put the CD back on the bar and thought of my brother Butch and his teenage fantasies of playing in a rock band. My parents gave him a guitar. He took lessons but I don't remember him playing much. His passion, if he really had one, receded once his fantasies clashed with his disinterest in practicing. In time his guitar gathered cobwebs. It has stood at a slant in a corner of his bedroom for years now, below a window where I can still see the log pile behind our house that he and Michael and I played in as kids. We'd creep up to it after school. Raccoons burrowed inside it during the day. We would shine flashlights into the cracks between the logs and watch multiple pockets of narrow eyes blink at us from the shadows. Most of the logs have now crumbled into splinters, and when it rains the remaining logs stand isolated like islands in a deepening pool of water.

The families living on Woodley Road then were mostly Irish. Over the years, my parents have noticed more Eastern Europeans and Asian couples moving in. According to my father, an Indian family lives not far from our house. Maybe Egyptian. He doesn't know which.

My parents and I finish the pizza. I take their plates and load the dishwasher. Pulsing red lights draw me to a window above the sink, and I see two police cars in the driveway of the Castle. My father and mother notice the lights too, and together we peer out the window toward the road, stare through the darkening evening and the outstretched branches of leafless trees.

"What now?" my father wonders.

"More vandalism?" my mother says. "A break-in, do you think?"

I doubt that anyone has broken into the Castle. Most of the houses on Woodley Road have complex security systems and motion sensors that blast the street with revolving floodlights when so much as a squirrel scampers across a lawn at night. My parents don't have those kinds of devices, but they've taken their own precautions against intruders.

When I was growing up, we never opened the door to someone we didn't know. The doorbell would ring and we all stopped whatever we were doing and froze in place. We shut off the TV and anything else that might reveal that we were home. My mother would whisper, "Don't make noise." My father would peek out a window. The doorbell would ring once, twice, three times. We listened to ourselves breathe, listened for the sound of footsteps retreating down the walk, for the sound of an engine starting and of a car leaving. We didn't budge. We absorbed the weighty silence left behind until my parents gave the all-clear. Then my father opened the front door, and like hunters we looked for a sign.

"Where're the police going?" my mother says. "Into the Castle?"

"Three police, that's a lot," my father notes.

A dog starts barking, but it sounds far off.

"What're the police doing now?" my mother asks.

"I don't know. They seem to be standing around," my father says.

One of the squad cars backs out of the driveway and leaves.

"Well, it looks like the police are going," my father reports.

"Yeah, they're getting in their cars," I say.

"What do you think happened?" my mother wonders.

"An alarm may have gone off by accident," I suggest.

"I bet he takes the association to court for whatever happened tonight," my father says. "I wish I hadn't signed that damned petition. This has gotten too personal. It's not him, it's his house I opposed."

An odd kind of emptiness hovers over the street after the police drive off. Then a pair of headlights tunnel up the road and a car turns into our driveway.

"Who can this be?" my father says.

"Don't answer the door," my mother commands.

I stare out the window until I recognize the car. "It's Michael," I say.

My parents look at me, surprised.

"Why's he here?" my mother says. "Is anything wrong?"

"No, no," I reassure them. "He called earlier, remember? Said he'd come by after dinner."

"Oh, yes," my father says in a drifting voice that tells me he does not remember. He hurries to the front door to let Michael in. I walk into the living room with my mother and we sit on the couch without speaking. I hear my father sort through the confusion of keys on his key chain.

Staring out the window at the backyard, I reach for my mother's hand. Woods seal us off from neighbors and the road, and the changes still to come from outside the perimeter of trees.

Stay a Little Longer

(2010)

I've been in Islamabad for nearly four weeks for the *Virginia Quarterly Review*. My editor asked me to cover the rise in violence from jihadi groups opposed to Pakistan's alliance with the United States. Every morning, before making my rounds to the various ministries for news updates and press conferences, before negotiating the countless bureaucratic hurdles required to see Minister So-and-So, I stop at a bakery near my guesthouse with my Pakistani colleagues Yassin and Tahir for bread and tea.

I met Yassin by chance in 2004, when I was in Pakistan for Knight Ridder Newspapers covering the search for Osama bin Laden. Yassin, a taxi driver, picked me up one morning. He asked in his limited English if I needed a driver for the day. I told him I did. I said I also needed a translator, and he suggested his brother-in-law, Tahir. The three of us teamed up for four weeks. When I left Pakistan, I kept in touch with Tahir by email. When *VQR* hired me for this trip, I coordinated with Tahir for us to work together again.

Yassin takes pride in driving for foreigners and insists on calling me *sir*, opening my door, and carrying my camera pack. Every time we park, he inspects his graying hair and pats down any stray strand. In contrast to the care he takes with his hair, he wears a worn *salaawr kameez* that is stained black in spots and appears to never have been washed.

Tahir, on the other hand, typically dresses in pressed blue jeans and muscle shirts. A man in his thirties, he lives with his parents, listens to American soft rock music, and ogles young women on the street like a horny teenager. Although he knows our morning routine, he always asks me, "Where're we going, boss?" Before I finish explaining, he cuts me off.

"Okay, okay, okay," he says. "I remember now."

We call each other Mr. Okay, Okay, our running joke.

The baker's name is Hanif. He sits cross-legged on the flour-dusted floor. His bakery overlooks a narrow street in the Aabpara neighborhood, where in the morning I see taxi drivers asleep, their sandaled feet sticking out open car windows. They rouse themselves from time to time and drive into downtown seeking fares. If they find none, they drift back to Hanif's shop for tea, bread, and another nap.

Beside Hanif, a black-haired boy beats mounds of dough into flat circles before he slaps them against the flame-seared walls of a clay-brick oven. The boy looks to be about eight years old. A thin coat of flour covers his loose-fitting clothes. He works barefoot, the soles of his feet black. He sweats from the heat of the oven and wipes his forehead. The aroma of baking bread rises around him and us, competing with odors already circulating on the awakening street: dew-damp garbage piles, diesel exhaust, the squawking of panicked chickens being carried upside down by boys to the bazaar.

I am pleased to see Hanif. For the past few days his shop has been closed. I'm returning to the States tomorrow, and while I don't pretend to know Hanif, his bakery has been a steady part of my morning routine. I didn't want to leave without dropping by one more time.

Something is different today, however. Hanif does not greet us with his usual hearty *Aslam alakum*. Instead, after we shake hands, he settles into a quiet posture that seems to shrink him in size.

Oh, well, I think, we all have bad days. I assume this is one of his. I am content to stand in silence and allow the morning to evolve around us.

When Hanif does speak to us, Tahir translates. "The bread will be ready soon," Hanif says in a voice barely above a whisper. He strokes his white beard, stained brown from tobacco. He turns to the boy and instructs him to take a sack of bread to a nearby Afghan restaurant.

When we first stopped here, Tahir told me that most of the people who live in Aabpara are Afghans. They fled here when the Russians invaded Afghanistan in 1979. Others arrived more recently, after 9/11. Today, however, with terrorist bombs exploding in their cities, Pakistanis have begun accusing their Afghan neighbors of bringing "their" war into Pakistan. The accusations have gone from finger-pointing to harassment.

As we wait for bread, Tahir translates some of the comments he overhears from Hanif's Afghan customers.

"If a bomb happens, the police stop us and ask, 'Who are you? Afghani? Yes?' If we don't hand over some money we are arrested," one man says.

"One day I was coming from Peshawar," another man says, "and I was pulled off at a checkpoint and arrested. I had to give them five hundred rupees before they would let me go."

"One time, the police took two thousand rupees from me," a third man says. "We can't move. We can't do anything."

Hanif nods, a sympathetic look creasing his face. He moved to Islamabad during "the Russian time" from his home in Wardak, not far from Kabul, he says. His vacant stare, though, tells me he is not really involved in the conversation. He wipes flour off his clothes and drags the back of a hand across his forehead. He yawns and I notice his missing teeth.

The customers see that he is preoccupied and drift off. One man looks back at Hanif and shakes his head. It is too bad about his wife,

Tahir hears him say. The other men nod. Hanif has two grown sons in Lahore, another man says, but that is a four-hour drive. The men frown. They continue talking, and I gather from what Tahir tells me that Hanif's wife died of a heart attack a few days ago, which explains why the bakery was closed and why he is so subdued now.

After the men leave, I ask Tahir to tell Hanif that I am sorry about his wife. Hanif nods his appreciation. He clasps his hands together and sighs.

"He says, 'She is with God,'" Tahir tells me.

Hanif watches Tahir translate. Then he looks up like someone startled and shouts to the boy, who darts through a curtain in back, revealing a hall that seems to lead into a house. Within minutes he returns with glass cups, a pot of tea, and a plate of cookies on a warped plastic tray. He sets them down by Hanif. Hanif pours green tea into the cups and hands the cups to Yassin, Tahir, and me. Tea leaves float in the cups. Hanif motions to the cookies and sets the plate near us.

"Thank you," I say.

I watch the boy slide a wooden paddle into the oven and flip the bread like a pancake.

"Who is he?" I ask.

My grandson, Hanif says. He works in the bakery before and after school.

I take a cookie and dunk it in my tea. I notice an elderly woman peering at me from behind a curtain. Gray hair falls to her shoulders. She stands stooped over a cane, and circles form hammocks beneath her eyes. Maybe Hanif's sister? I wonder. She leans forward on her cane and I see a hump on her back and think of my mother, who also has a hump caused by curvature of the spine. It's a cruel deformity for my mother, who always seemed taller than she was because of her erect posture.

"Straighten up," she'd say, poking Butch, Michael, and me in our backs when we were kids. "You'll be all hunched when you're older." I'm fifty-two now, and her jabs made an impression. I carry myself as straight as she once did. Chest out, shoulders back. Odd, the impressions that stick with us from childhood. My mother will see soon enough how well I listened to her. When I leave Pakistan, I'll pack up my Kansas City apartment and then drive to Winnetka to live with her.

My father died last year, which precipitated my impending move. On a spring day, while shopping at a Mariano's Supermarket, he slipped and fell in the parking lot and broke his hip. He was ninety-four. The surgery went well but a week later, at a rehabilitation center, problems developed. My father refused to eat hospital food. He didn't like it and that was that. His blue polka-dot hospital smock began drooping off him like a coat too big for its hanger. Fluid started filling his lungs. His heart and kidneys stopped functioning properly. The antibiotics doctors gave him helped one organ but damaged others. I called him the night before he was put on a ventilator but did not recognize his voice. He sounded like someone talking underwater. I came home.

My father remained on the ventilator for three days while doctors drained his lungs. He died May 31, 2009, four days after the ventilator was removed. My mother moved in with my brother Michael.

Two months before my father died I had been laid off by the *Kansas City Star*, a casualty of the Great Recession. After a year of freelancing, I was barely covering my rent. I decided to return to Winnetka and care for my mother. She couldn't stay with Michael forever, and a nursing home was out of the question. *Pop is dead, Mom, and now we're putting you in a home.* Michael and I agreed we couldn't do that. If I moved to Winnetka, she could return home. I assumed I'd stay a few months, arranging home health-care services for her while at the same time slashing my expenses and getting back on my feet. That was my plan.

Before I flew to Pakistan I contacted elder-care agencies and explained that my mother would need someone to help with cooking and cleaning, plus a driver to take her to the supermarket and doctor appointments. Ideally, I said, she would form relationships with her caregivers, who in turn would provide companionship. Anything is possible, I was told. It just depends how much you're willing to spend.

Then I left for Pakistan.

A burly man with a heavy beard stops by the bakery, his cracked, rubber sandals slapping loudly against the pavement.

"*Assalamu alaikum*," the man says in a loud voice.

"*Assalamu alaikum*," Hanif replies.

I push the tray toward the man and he helps himself to a cookie. The boy fetches another cup and Hanif pours the man tea. The man begins talking. I pester Tahir about what he's saying.

"This is a nation of absconders, Hanif," the man says. He pauses, sips his tea. "You can't stop the police. When my family and I came here in 2003, it was not too bad. Now it is much worse. Everywhere there are the police. I don't care about the Taliban. I am just worried about policemen." He finishes his cookie, washing it down with another slurp of tea. Then he shakes Hanif's hand and wanders over to the taxi drivers, who have moved from one shady spot to another.

It strikes me that Hanif did not match the man's story about the police with one of his own. I mention this to Tahir and Tahir asks Hanif about his experiences with the authorities. About a year and a half ago, Hanif says, a police officer stopped by the bakery. The oven was heating and Hanif sent the boy to buy flour. He told the officer he would not have any bread until later. The officer said he did not want bread. He told Hanif that beginning that evening, Hanif would give him one thousand rupees—about eleven dollars—every night. If Hanif refused, the police officer could not guarantee protection from vandals. The officer said it was the least Hanif could do, since the war in Afghanistan was causing problems for all of Pakistan and the police in particular. Two of his fellow officers had been killed by suicide bombers at their checkpoint. "You endanger my life," the police officer said. "I am newly married and want to have a family. If I am gone, what will my wife do?"

Hanif knew he had no choice. God only knew what the police might do to his bakery if he resisted. That night and every night thereafter, at 8:30 p.m. Hanif met the police officer a block from the bakery with the thousand rupees in hand. Eventually their meetings became as much a part of Hanif's life as awakening at sunrise when the mullahs called the faithful to prayer. Hanif was never late for their nightly rendezvous. He began to look forward to seeing the policeman in the same way he anticipated talking to his regular morning customers. They asked each other about their families and shared the latest gossip about politicians or Bollywood movie stars. They wondered how much longer winter would last and argued about their favorite cricket teams. Hanif considered himself a customer of the police officer. As his customers paid him daily for his bread, Hanif paid the police officer nightly for his protection.

Hanif even went to meet the officer the evening his wife died. He did so out of a sense of obligation, but also perhaps to abandon for a few minutes the claustrophobic sadness that had descended on his home. When the policeman saw Hanif's grief-stricken face, he asked what was wrong. Hanif explained that his wife had died. The officer said he was very sorry and offered his condolences. He was surprised that Hanif had kept their appointment. Of course, there would have been consequences had he not, he said. He could not have known the circumstances that had kept Hanif away; he would only have thought that Hanif no longer wanted his bakery protected.

Hanif said he understood.

The officer said again how very sorry he was for Hanif's loss.

Hanif thanked him, then leaned against the car and said nothing for a while.

The officer smoked a cigarette and drummed his fingers against the dashboard. "I don't want to keep you," the officer said finally.

Hanif gave him his money and watched the officer stuff it in his breast pocket. Then Hanif handed him a five-hundred-rupee bill and asked him to stay a little longer. Hanif enjoyed leaning against the car, the rumble of its engine vibrating the metal against his body, the smell of the officer's cigarette, the quiet night around him in the glow of a streetlight.

The officer took the money and gave Hanif a few more minutes of his time. They did not talk. Finally, the policeman said he had to leave. Hanif gave him another five-hundred-rupee bill. He ended up giving the man three thousand additional rupees, until he insisted he had to go home and refused to take any more of Hanif's money. Hanif watched him drive away. Then he walked back to his home and to the sadness that awaited him there.

The next night Hanif waited for the officer at the usual time, but he did not show up then, or thereafter.

"We knew each other well," Hanif tells Tahir. "I was his customer and we were friends. I always gave him his money, but he did not oppress me for being Afghan and causing problems for his country."

I look at my watch. I have work to do and a full day of travel tomorrow. Among other things, I need to check my email and confirm my flight. I will travel more than twenty-four hours before I land in Washington and catch a plane for Kansas City.

I'll stay in Kansas City about four weeks, wrapping up loose ends, before I return to Winnetka. Then I'll interview people from various elder-care agencies. How much per hour? Do I pay for mileage if they take my mother to the doctor? Am I expected to provide them lunch and dinner? And on and on. I should write down my questions so I don't forget anything. There's so much, I realize, that I can't anticipate. I rub my neck. I'm thinking too much.

I finish my tea and push away the plate of cookies. The boy slings a sheet filled with fat pancake-shaped loaves of bread over a shoulder. He pauses on his way out to give me one. The warmth from the bread seeps into my fingers. I crack it open and close my eyes against the released heat. Hanif hands me newspaper to wrap it.

Leaving the bakery, the boy walks toward the bazaar, kicking at stones. The bread-filled sheet bounces against his back as if nothing else matters. Watching him, I imagine that the policeman is now blackmailing someone else. I bet he works this new guy for just a few weeks, long enough to make some money, short enough so that he doesn't get to know him. He doesn't need complications. He will move on to someone else.

But it shouldn't be complicated once I have the people in place for my mother. Still, I worry that I'm getting pulled into something that won't let me go; that I'll be involved in a process that never ends. That something will always need my attention. I won't be able to just up and leave one day.

"Good-bye," I tell Hanif as Tahir translates. "I return to the States tomorrow morning. I'll miss our mornings together."

"When will you be back in Pakistan?" Hanif says.

"I don't know."

He starts pouring tea into my cup. I put out my hand to stop him and tea splashes my fingers. I shake it off before it burns.

"No, no. Thank you," I say. "I have to go."

Hanif stares past me toward where the boy has gone, but he is no longer in sight. The taxi drivers and the glut of loitering men have also left. He takes a rag and wipes the spilled tea, then returns to the corner where he has spent most of the morning.

I start walking back to my guesthouse, the bread tucked under my arm. It has cooled quickly and lost its enticing aroma. I almost stop and look back to tell Hanif again that I'm sorry about his wife, but I decide against it. He will offer me more tea. I don't need more tea.

Before I Knew My Father
(2010)

I moved back home on March 1, 2010.

A stale odor permeated the living room, an odor I associated with the old people I had worked with when I was in social services. Air no longer circulated. I opened windows. A few were swollen shut, and all of them were gray with dust.

I began cleaning the house. I started by clearing months-old piles of papers off the breakfast nook table. It was here that my father had attempted to help me with the story problems I consistently failed in grammar-school math.

"Sally has three apples, Jane has four," my father read. "If Jane eats half of her apples and Sally eats one fourth of one of her apples, how many apples are left?"

The answer lay before my father as distinct as a diamond, and he jabbed the math book with his pencil while I bungled one answer after another, until the point of his pencil broke off and he could no longer contain himself.

"How many, how many, how many?" he would demand while I quivered beside him.

Finally, he'd give me the answer just to be done with it and slammed the math book shut, disgusted with me and, I think now, his own thin patience. I retreated to my bedroom.

My father listened to me go. He could not bring himself to

apologize, especially when he thought I wasn't trying. "That's your problem," he would say, "a lack of application." Next time, I imagine him saying to himself, he would control his temper and Malcolm would show effort.

I swept the papers off the table into a trash bag. "Sorry, Pop," I said.

I moved on to my father's study, where stacks of unopened mail obscured his desk. Framed diplomas from the University of Wisconsin and the Harvard Business School hung on the wall. An adding machine still registered the last figures he had tapped in. The 1946 Remington typewriter he used sat on an end table. He had taken one computer lesson, as I recall, but the mouse and the dancing arrow it controlled frustrated him, and he returned to his typewriter. He never changed the ribbon, just banged the keys harder as the type grew fainter and fainter.

I opened a desk drawer and leafed through some envelopes. Bank statements. Canceled checks. Business letters. All arranged by date. All of them years old, predating the time when simple tasks became too much.

In another drawer I found envelopes postmarked July and August 1948. They were addressed in my father's strong, sprawling handwriting to my mother at a New Jersey address where she had stayed for a summer with her sister Elvira.

Sunday—
Dearest Letty—
Hi darling—I love you more and more and miss you much more every day. It seems like you have been gone for months. Please write often and miss me a little too. I am lost without you here.

Love letters.

My parents met in Puerto Rico in 1945. My father, a first lieu-tenant in the navy, was stationed there. They first saw each other at a dance party. My father tapped her partner on the shoulder and cut in. He was wearing his white uniform with lieutenant's bars. He had a slim, muscular build, dark hair slicked and parted to one side. He spoke and moved with confidence, holding my mother close, his dark eyes searching her face. They danced near the beach on a patio. A live band played above the soft sound of ocean waves rolling in and the rhythmic call of coquí frogs. My father put one hand on her waist and led her through a jazz tune. She had no other partners that night. They exchanged phone numbers, and my father called her the next day. By the time she left Puerto Rico three months later, they had, as my mother put it, "an understanding."

They married in New York City on a muggy June morning in 1947 in a chapel in St. Patrick's Cathedral, and spent their honeymoon on Nantucket. They lived in Chicago until 1957, when they moved to Winnetka. My father administered the Midwest office of Perfecto Garcia Cigars, a business founded in 1905 by his father and his three uncles, the oldest of whom was named Perfecto. At its peak, Perfecto Garcia Cigars employed twelve hundred people. My uncle Manuel managed the Tampa factory. According to my mother, my father had wanted to start his own company, she had no idea what kind—it was more of a notion, she said, an undefined ambition—but his father told him to join the family business. "If my father said jump, I didn't ask why, I asked how high," my father used to say.

When my brothers and I were growing up, my mother would take us to his third-floor office on South Wells Street. The elevator doors opened to a dank space with a gray tile floor, four desks and two large windows with their view blocked by a brick building bearing a Coca-Cola sign. A poster above my father's desk bore an illustration of a mustachioed man gripping a thick stogie and declaring beneath a Perfecto Garcia sign, *What this country needs is a good* $1.25 *cigar*! The acrid odor of tobacco wafted through the air as the noise of passing L trains drowned our voices.

I recall one elderly man, Otto, who had worked for my grandfather and now my father. He had short white hair and wore glasses. He carried a clipboard and scurried from one desk to the next with the energy of someone much younger. Otto rarely spoke but always had a twinkle in his eyes and a grin on his face when he looked in my direction. Another man, Jack, sat behind a desk. He also wore glasses. They were balanced on the end of his nose and sometimes slipped off. The ceiling lights played off his bald head. He liked to show Butch, Michael, and me the math equations he loved to solve, much as Otto enjoyed crossword puzzles that we couldn't fathom.

Perfecto Garcia Cigars used Cuban tobacco until the embargo in 1962. My father and Manuel found another tobacco source, but according to my mother it took a long time, and the company lost revenue. Competition from emerging chain stores also hurt the business. I remember hearing my father argue with Manuel over the phone about how to improve sales. When they finished talking, my father would slam the phone down and sit in the breakfast nook, legs crossed, tapping the air furiously with his foot and biting his knuckles.

When I was about to graduate from college in 1979, my father and Manuel sold the business at a loss and retired. I rarely heard my father mention it again. He was sixty-five. His Harvard diploma gathered dust. I wonder now if he thought of that imagined business he had wanted to start, if he even looked at his degree or asked himself what his dreams had all been for, given how things turned out.

As a family, we went along as if nothing had happened. Our lives didn't change. We had a roof over our heads, three meals a day and still took vacations. We weren't hurting, is what I'm saying. Externally, anyway.

Internally? Well, we had never been a "talky" family. We didn't go to one another with our problems. We had no intimate conversations. My brothers and I knew to keep our left hand on our laps when we ate and to say thank you and no thank you. We did not confide our fears and joys in one another. We weren't that kind of family. I don't know why. I presume my parents were raised in a similarly remote manner. What all this means is that when my father sold the business, whatever he felt, he felt it alone. His temper grew shorter. He paced the house. He sat by himself. It was uncomfortable to be around him, but I wouldn't say we suffered. Discomfort, avoidance, those can mean many things, but suffering isn't among them. Not financial suffering anyway.

Decades earlier, my father had indulged in a fantasy about buying a ranch. That desire began when we visited Colorado in 1966. I was nine. As a family we all fell in love with the craggy Rocky Mountains covered with trees and the snowcapped peaks spread unevenly against the sky. My father watched men in cowboy hats pass us in their pickup trucks. He watched them riding on horseback, rocking with the movement of their mounts. He thrust his face into cool breezes. He took in the clean air and felt refreshed.

Back home, my mother drew the living room curtains to keep sunlight from fading the sofa and two swivel chairs. My father and I sat in the dark with the end table lamp on and read glossy sales brochures about dozens of ranches he had requested from Colorado real estate companies. I imagined lassoing cattle and heating branding irons red hot. I'd wear cowboy boots and jeans and red plaid shirts, and I'd learn to shoot. I'd ride a horse. I wouldn't attend school.

My father and I reviewed brochures almost every weekend for months. It took a long time, but I slowly realized that our dream would go no farther than our living room. The accumulated excuses month after month for why he would not buy this ranch or that one quashed my nine-year-old fantasies of becoming a cowboy. I realized that we weren't moving. My father, however, maintained the pretense, but without me. He sat alone in the living room, the lamp on in the darkness, until he too stopped pretending.

During the fourteen years I lived in San Francisco, I'd come home to visit about once a year. Over dinner, I talked about my work at the Ozanam Center. One evening, I mentioned that only one percent of our clientele got off the street.

"Any business with those kinds of numbers would close its doors," my father said. He put down his fork and left the table for the couch, crossed his arms, and stared at me in disgust.

"You're a goddamned idiot," he said.

When I started reporting from Kabul in 2001, my father expressed surprise when I told him that with its rugged mountains and vast expanses of barren land, Afghanistan reminded me of the American West. In the States, I told him, the glow from city lights illuminate the sky, but in Afghanistan, a country without power in many places, the night sky is a deep, tar-rich black. I could read by the light of the moon and stars.

"Now, that would be something," he said.

I saw my father when Butch died in 2006 and again about four months later. I sat across from him in the breakfast nook on a Saturday morning eating breakfast. When I finished my coffee, I got up to take a walk. My father asked to come with me.

As we left the driveway we saw a man in a suit and tie inspecting flowers in his yard. "My father wore a suit and tie every day, even weekends, just like that guy," my father said.

"Why don't you have a photograph of him?" I asked. "You have one of Granny but not your father."

He didn't answer. We'd walked about a block farther when he told me to stop. "I'm tired," he said. "You can go on."

"Okay," I replied. I watched him walking back to the house, bent over, pumping his arms in his rapid, nervous way of walking, and it bothered me seeing him alone. I went back with him. When we reached the driveway, he said, "I don't know why I don't have a picture of my father. That's a good question."

Nearly a year has passed since my father died, and my brief time at home has changed everything. Women from a home health-care service come by throughout the day and take my mother to church and help her with breakfast, lunch, and dinner before they go out again on an errand or help my mother get ready for bed. "Have a good sleep," my mother will say to me on her way up the stairs.

Once a week a cleaning woman dusts, vacuums, and mops her way through the house, and painters have been hired, and a gardener mows the yard every Friday. Each evening I sort the mail. It doesn't pile up.

I've wondered whether my parents were unaware of the extent of the deterioration that had claimed the house. I concluded it was more complicated than that. Toward the end of his life, my father was tired, his fatigue brought on by a long life. He was tired because the human battery was winding down, lights were shutting off, circuits breaking, never to be recharged. I imagine he was too exhausted to bother with maintaining the house. *I'll get to it in a minute,* he thought.

Slowly papers began stacking up. Dust collected. Mildew flecked the walls. He would get to it. Eventually, tables were completely covered with unopened mail and newspapers. "Don't touch it," I imagine him telling my mother. "I'll get to it." She was losing her sight and her back was giving her problems. "Leave it, Letty. I'll do it later."

The piles got bigger too. He considered the amount of time required to sort through each one but he was tired. He would get to it all, he convinced himself. In a minute. In a minute.

I don't miss my father. I miss not missing him. Sometimes I reread the love letters he sent my mother and think of the young man who wrote them and with whom my mother fell in love and married.

Wednesday—

There is a gale blowing over this desk at the moment. I have the west window open and its wonderful although a little on the breezy side. I love you and miss you. Love, Chuck.

Lately I've begun recalling moments with him when I was very young. Summer vacation. I am six and in a pool with my father at a Bermuda hotel. Rain pours down. We duck under the water together and look up. The rain pellets the surface. We come up for air and my father says, "You saw the footsteps of hundreds of elves running across the water." I laugh. My mother shouts from a window, concerned about lightning. My father grins. "We are risk takers," he tells me.

My father would be pleased that I moved home to look after my mother. Her well-being would have meant more to him than his displeasure at the money I've spent fixing the house.

I try not to think about that, to engage in an argument between us that will never occur. Instead, at night, when my mother has gone to bed, I sit alone in his study in front of his typewriter and focus on his approval, a first step, I think, toward missing him.

Walking

(2016)

Weekday mornings I see children all bundled up, strolling out of driveways, book bags thrown over shoulders. They look younger than I was when my mother finally allowed me to walk to school.

"You're not old enough," my mother told me when I was six and asked to join my friends. "I don't care what your friends' parents allow them to do," she said. "You're not their son."

Her concerns were no different from those of any other mother. She wanted to be confident that I'd be careful crossing streets, that I wouldn't talk to strangers, get lost, or do any number of things that parents worry about. With the benefit of hindsight, I suspect that my mother was also reluctant to let go of her youngest child. I was in a hurry. I wanted to walk to school sooner rather than later. Eventually I found a way to do it without waiting for my mother's permission.

Elm trees and dense woods encircled our property. My brothers pointed out trees with branches bent down to the ground that they said had been tied off as trail markers by Indian war parties. I imagined certain dirt paths were ancient trails that wound through woods that were all dusky shadows and splashes of sunlight until they emerged from the trees and became highways unfurling toward the interstate.

The woods were my ally. The bushes at the end of our driveway obscured me when the school bus stopped to pick me up. My mother, keeping an eye on me from the kitchen window as I waited, could see me approach the bus but not get on it. One morning, when the bus driver opened the door to take me to the third grade, I told him I was walking. As he drove off, I darted into the woods and onto a path.

Alone, I made my way to school, careful not to be noticed when the path twisted around a neighbor's backyard. I could see the family eating breakfast through the glass doors of their living room. I was free of restrictions but scared, sure that somehow my mother would find out. My breathing sounded very loud. Leaves crunched underfoot and I shuddered at the noise. I looked behind me, certain someone was there. I hurried on, the dense brush restricting my movement, until I broke through and reached the road in front of Avoca East Elementary School. It was early and the sun had not yet cleared the tall brick building. I crossed the street and joined the mayhem of children scrambling out of a bus and ran with them through the parking lot into the school.

I didn't walk to school every morning. I wanted to, but I worried that if I did, the bus driver would eventually stop coming by and his absence would give me away. Once or twice every couple of weeks, however, I'd tell him to go on without me, and then I'd disappear into the woods.

When I was ten and entered the fifth grade, my mother allowed me to walk to school. I don't know why. My brothers had had to wait until sixth grade. Perhaps I had worn her down; certainly I was persistent. Or perhaps she had finally accepted that there would be no more children after me, and that holding on to me would never fill that void, because she could not prevent me from growing up.

I sauntered out of our driveway and onto the road in full view of everyone, swinging my arms as if nothing else mattered. I looked back and saw my mother watching, her face small in the kitchen window. I waved. The sounds of my footsteps bounced off the pavement. I smelled cut grass drying in trash bags. I overheard people talking as they stood by their idling cars. Some waved, glancing at their watches. Dogs barked and ran to the ends of driveways before being called back. I kicked at stones. I walked on, following the road.

That day after school, I determined that I would leave home when I was old enough. It would be an impossibly long wait, I knew, until I was an adult and free to do as I pleased. Once the moment arrived, however, I wouldn't delay a second longer. I told my mother of my plans.

"That's a fine how-do-you-do," she said.

I kept my word and left home at eighteen. I could not have imagined I'd return at fifty-three to care for my mother.

After she died, her body was cremated. Her urn stands beside my father's on a table in the living room of our empty house beside a photograph of Butch. My parents will soon be interred in Santa Maria Magdalena de Pazzis cemetery in Old San Juan, where my mother's family is buried.

Michael and I have yet to sell the house. I'm glad. I'll miss it when it's gone.

I still live in Kansas City. I freelance and work temp jobs when I don't. I'm used to living this way. The furniture I brought with me from my parents' house includes the kitchen table, the one on which I first wrote to Dale Titler. His letters and the letters from Alfred Franklyn, H. E. Hart, Rupert Radecki, and other World War I veterans fill a box in my closet. I don't recall all the details of Richthofen's final flight anymore. I concluded long ago that it was not important who shot him down. His short life made the Red Baron the stuff of legend. Now he is lost to me within the meandering contours of my own life, lost so often on journeys that at times seemed to lead nowhere but in their own way, and with their own veiled reasons, have brought me to this moment.

The habits of my parents have become mine. I awaken at 5:45 in the morning as they did, and walk my dogs. A few joggers share the silence. Far off I hear the wheeze of commuter buses gathering volume. The humid fragrance of watered lawns hovers around me this spring morning. Inside some houses I see the outlines of people shuffling around their kitchens. Through open windows I hear the chatter of television programs announcing the latest traffic and weather reports.

The street twists around Troost Park, looming out of the dark beneath fogged streetlights. Shadows cling to me and stretch away as my dogs and I submerge ourselves in the tall grass, tramping a path toward a stand of white oak. The woods beckon. I hear only the crunch of dry leaves beneath our feet. We move beyond the fringe of lights and the constraints of the dawning world around us.

Acknowledgments

My sincere thanks to all the staff at Skyhorse Publishing, especially editor Caroline Russomanno for working with me on this book. Additionally, my thanks to former Skyhorse editor Jerrod MacFarlane for taking on this project in the first place.

To the many friends and colleagues who read and critiqued these essays. I especially want to acknowledge Jesse Barker, Eve Talbot, Chris Jerome, Heather World, Scott Canon, Chuck Murphy, Roland Sharillo, Susan Curtis, Joanne Fish, Lucian K. Truscott IV, and Dale Maharidge.

For Sandy Weiner who experienced many of these stories with me and encouraged me to write them down.

Finally, my gratitude to the Titler family for welcoming me into their home and sharing details about Dale. He remains for me, as does my brother Butch, a guiding light.